Fierce

an anthology of dynamic new
queer monologues for actors

Published May 2022 by Team Angelica Publishing,
an imprint of Angelica Entertainments Ltd

Team Angelica Publishing
51 Coningham Road
London W12 8BS

TEAM
ANGELICA

www.teamangelica.com
A CIP catalogue record for this book is available from
the British Library

ISBN 978-1-916-3561-4-6

Supported using public funding by
**ARTS COUNCIL
ENGLAND**

LOTTERY FUNDED

Disclaimer/Reclaimer

It's weird, after years of teaching so many actors to write business letters that avoid over-using the words 'I', 'Me' and 'My', if at all, to now be writing these forewords infested with I, I, I. But you know what? Even though this trilogy of books have been lovingly assembled as heartfelt offerings to the reader, and as showcases for the 200 brilliant writers who have poured themselves into every word, it's become so clear to me, me, me, that that this project, this labour of love, in which every word is written by someone else - is deeply personal.

I used to say, 'I don't want to be a black writer. Or a gay writer. Or a working class writer. I just want to be a writer.' Now I look back and think why not? Why did I think that being flavourless was radical? Why was I denying my herbs and spices? Why did I think my various perspectives and nuances were a distraction or deficit? Lots of writers think that way. Actors too. But who we are is not a limitation. It's a launch pad. It's an advantage. And lots of emerging creatives seem to be realising that fact more and more. Actors call out on social media for audition/showcase speeches that they can relate to. They write me emails asking for recommendations for working class monologues, LGBTQIA+ monologues, black, brown, Asian monologues. And more. I give them what I've written. But it's not enough. Try as I might, I haven't written enough or read enough to cover all the bases, to offer up all the nuances. What's needed is more writers.

And so we put out a call on social media for emerging writers (many of whom are actors themselves) who'd like to be mentored on how to write a great audition speech for queer actors, working class actors and/or underrepresented ethnicities... And so, six months and countless phone/WhatsApp feedback sessions later, we have these three books: *Fierce*, *Common* and *Lit*. Every speech is 3 minutes or less. Each one has its own attitude and vibe. Posh black voices, rural gay voices, educated council estate voices, stereotypes and anti-stereotypes and everything in between. Voices as various and complex as yours. This collection of speeches is for you. They're meant to be said, not read. Read 'em out loud. Whisper them. Shout them. Stretch them. Sing them. Bring them to life. Smash the audition. Stop the show. Be as gay or ethnic as you feel like being. Code switch. Nuance. Clarify. Enlighten. Challenge. Confuse. And if nothing between these covers does the business for you... write your own.

Rikki Beadle-Blair

Fierce Thoughts

A friend asked me write a play for them once, based on an idea they had, about a band that didn't make it having a reunion years later. When discussing their journeys, I suggested one of them had come out as a gay and he rolled his eyes and said, 'You're obsessed.' And he challenged me to write a play with no gay characters. I told him to shove his challenge. Not because I didn't want to write a play with no visibly gay characters, I do that regularly. But because there would be nothing wrong with me if every single character I wrote or acted was queer. That I could do so a million times and never repeat myself; that queerness is a more than a rainbow, it's a kaleidoscope. And that his frustration with my passion is his own problem. My unashamed passion for LGBTQIA+ inclusion is one of my strengths. Your queerness, whether it's one drop of you or your entire bloodstream is a strength. It's not an indulgence. It's not a hinderance. It's not a limitation. And this book is a testament to that. There's a huge range of representations, here, butch queers, fem queers, out queers, closet queers, black queers, brown queers, woke queers, self-loathing queers, jaded queers, idealistic queers, healthy queers, sick queers, posh queers, common queers, queers who hate the word queer and queers who celebrate it. And it barely touches the surface. So I guess we'll have to do more books, then. But until we do, feast on this. Feast on our fabulousness. This is a buffet. You are a banquet, savour your flavours. Go out and smash that audition, showcase or showreel with your complex alphabetic rainbow self. The world needs you on that stage or screen or sound waves in all your moods and shades. Show 'em what you're made of. Be subtle, be blatant, be complicated and contradictory. Be flaming. Be boy or girl or non-binary-neighbour next door. Be fierce.

Rikki

Table of Contents

A Country Gay Left Home Alone
by Alex Britt

Liam   Right – we haven't got long.

Usually if he goes out it's for about an hour – that's how long his walks are – which means I can just about squeeze in the next episode of *Drag Race*. If I time it right. But it's a risky one. Cos it's happened before that he's come back and he's stumbled in – cos he doesn't knock – and he's stumbled in on Ru, the girls and I... I can't take the look of disappointment anymore – I think he'd actually prefer to catch me watching straight porn. Literally, watching Pornhub.com, out in the open on the big screen TV, with girls and their... *tig ol' bitties*... doing whatever... *tig ol' bitties* do, I guess, but – yeah, he'd rather that than catch me watching Ru's queens lip-syncing the house down.

His house. Down. *To the ground.*

And, if I'm honest, there's been more than one occasion where I've started to join in and I've actually felt the walls begin to shake, you know? Lip-syncing is sort of my speciality – you get good at it when you can't sing along to *Born This Way* at fourteen so you have to mime it instead – but, anyway! Yes, I've got to get it all out now, before he comes back. So, here goes...

'YAAAAAS KWEEN, WERK, MAMA, BITCH!'

Ugh, that feels good.

Maybe he's gone shopping… that would give me two hours…

Two *fucking hours!* I could listen to Mariah Carey's incredible sophomore hit album *Emotions.* Twice! Again!

I like attempting her whistle runs – she's so phenomenal – here, listen: '*Make me feel, soooooooooo uhua-uhua-uhua-aaaaaaaaaaaaaa–*'

Or! Or! Or! I could watch *God's Own Country.* Or *Moonlight.*

OR MOST OF *CALL ME BY YOUR NAME.* SHIT THIS IS BIG.

Okay. Calm down, Liam, or you'll waste this time, and there's nothing worse than wasting *this* time. Where you can just *be.* Unapologetic. As much as possible. You don't have to hide anymore. Cos there's only so many times you can pretend to still like football, like, *ugh, YEAH MAN, what a great GOAL, ugh!* in a day without going crazy, right? But whenever it's mentioned on the telly – the gay thing, not the football thing – or when it's part of a film, or on the news even, it's just like… a punch to the gut. Like someone's poured ice down my back and taken a shit in my mouth and – and, yeah, it's just so uncomfortable. Cos I know he's sat there next to me, thinking about it too. Thinking about me. Who I am. Who I could have been. Thinking, *Why can't he be like Simon across the road, he's got a girlfriend and a normal life and –?*

And, yes, I know he *tries* to hide his shame, but he's not as good at it as me, so... whenever he is in the house, it's like this grey cloud is over us constantly... and... and this time – *my time* – it just lets the sun shine. For a little bit.

So! Okay, Kween – let's do this! Heads for Mariah, tails for Timmy C –

Wait.

No, false alarm. He was only saying hi to Sue next door.

Sorry, Timmy. Maybe next time.

A Missed Call Away
by Ashling O'Shea

Jamie *(tipsy in a toilet)* I think I've fancied every woman
I've ever met. Now I know that sounds crazy, and I'm
not doing a lot for our 'just because I'm a queer
woman doesn't mean I fancy you' fight. But I'm being
serious. Every time I meet a woman, I imagine what it
would be like to fuck them. Okay, maybe with some
people I think about it for ten seconds, cringe, throw
up a bit in my mouth and move on... but there's still
those ten seconds!

I've fancied every woman I've ever met. Except you.
Dunno why. You're amazing. You're beautiful. Funny.
Smart. Kind. But I never thought about it. You've just
always been there, you know? My go-to gal. My
'make you piss yourself laughing but still tell you
when you're being a cunt' gal. My 'steal someone's
booze and lock ourselves in the toilet of a party' gal.

My 'pick up all the pieces and put me back together
again' gal.

I remember when I told you about my aunty killing
herself. How it broke me. 'Cause that's what that
kinda thing does. It takes a part of your heart and
turns it into this cancerous lump of guilt and regret.
How it burns when you realise you haven't spoken to
a friend in a while, or when your gut tells you someone's hiding their pain from you.

4

Or every fucking time you get a missed call. And you only ever text me after that. You said you saw my heart fall out of my arse every time I got a missed call and you never wanted to scare me like that.

There was this one night we were in my back garden, chain-smoking and playing chess. We have some weird drunk habits, huh? You were taking ages to move and I'd already started sweating out vodka, so I nudged you and said I'd projective over the board if you didn't hurry the fuck up.

You moved your bishop, leaving your queen completely unprotected.
And you just – stared at it. You asked, 'Do you ever think it'd be easier if you took your piece out of the equation? If you just gave it up?'
I can't even remember what I mumbled back. Probably something about you not needing to give up because I was gunna thrash you anyway. So I took your queen and a move later finished the game. Then I went to bed. I just went to bed. I should have –
Funny that the one person I've never fancied is the only one I've ever loved.

And you never did call.
You never gave me the chance to pick up.

I hate you for that.
And I love you for that.

Amanda
by André Fialho

AMANDA is standing in high heels with two police officers in front of her. One is Charles, the other is 'Bertha'.

Amanda   Yes, I am a drag queen but please, no 'yas gurl!', 'Come through queen!', 'Okrrrr!', I hate that shit! 'Specially from two straight white people.

I am just assuming, based on haircuts and skin condition.

I know him, but I can't remember your name... Can I call you Bertha? No? Your face is telling me no... Anyway!

Listen officers, I am deeply sorry, I have learnt my lesson, it was wrong of me to urinate in a public road, next to a primary school, up against your police car, but I was drunk... And desperate... And for the record, I am even more sorry for trying to resist your arrest, Bertha... I am so glad the nose bleeding stopped.

Pause. Looking only at Charles.

Listen... There is nothing I can say that will make this situation better. I know that these conditions are not ideal for us to meet again after all these years, but there are only two things we can do. You can give me my phone call, so I can ask my friend

Cupcake to come down here, pay my fine so I can go home, and we might never have to talk again. Or you look me straight in the eyes, I drop the drag queen act, you drop the cop act and we talk. Which one do you want, dad? Dad? ...Daddy?

Anjali and Sufi On the Eiffel Tower
by Sita Thomas

Anjali   Wahooo!!!! We made it! The Eiffel Tower! La Tour
Eiffel! I can't believe it! Aaaaaooooooooo!!!!

Oh my gosh don't you feel like you could just fly off
here? Like if these railings didn't exist we could just
lean forward and... wooosh! I'd fly up and draw a
massive heart in the French sky like I was a fire-
work. Just for you.

You're such a scaredy cat. Look at you, shaking like
a leaf. Hold on. I love you.

You're right – Je t'adore tu! I didn't get very far with
the Learning French app before we got here.

Can you believe it's been two years? Two years
since we met. The biggest whirlwind romance. Typi-
cal lesbians, moving in after one date! But so not
stereotypical in any other way... Hindu and Muslim.
Who'd have thought that 730 days after me sliding
into your DMs we'd be standing here right now.

So much against us. Yet our force is undeniable. It is
undeniable that I am meant to be with you. Now
I'm shaking.

So many times I've been scared in this. Scared the

first time I wanted to kiss you. Scared of losing family. Scared of what the world would think. Over and over, on and on. But the love we share is so much stronger than all of that. It transcends everything. Every time.

So much to overcome. And I know I'm in a totally different position than you in terms of my family – our family – and that everything that happened with yours –

I know you don't like to talk about it. But I just want you to know that I know how much of a sacrifice you made. And that my family is your family now.

You're right, it's not a sacrifice to be true to who you are... But it is brave. It's the bravest thing – you're the bravest thing. and I'm proud of you. I'm proud to be your girlfriend.

Attention, Paris! I'M IN LOVE WITH SUFI MALIK!!!

I can't stop smiling at you, the sparkle in your eyes, the wind in your hair, look at you. You're the kurta to my lehenga. My love for you could light up this entire tower. And Sufi... I want to know... will you...

Anjali goes down on one knee.

Will you?

Black (And)...
by Amber Sinclair-Case

AALIAY – early 20s, female identifying, Scottish.

Aaliya Black and Scottish.

Black and 21.

Black and a woman.

Black and queer.

I'm trained.

We're trained,

To say Black *just.*

Black *but.*

And whilst my butt is capable of standing alone,

That's not the point of this presentation.

Our assignment was to write about the world.

How we exist.

But when I'm assigned this world at birth from trained eyes

That 'see no colour'?

This world I'm assigned to becomes smaller.

Less than.

Black just.

So in this presentation, I will use

Black *and.*

Because in my world I can be Black and Scottish.

I can be Black and a doctor.

I can be Black *and* without being

Just black.

The intersection of identity

Goes beyond the colour you 'don't see'.
This beautiful, chocolate existence
Meets at crossroads, inconsistent
With the years of oppression linked to my skin.

Beat.

The first time my cold eyes lit up in flames
At the sheer beauty of another human?
It was a woman.
Helena Bonham Carter, to be exact.
(In *Sweeney Todd*)
I can't remember if it was the way her matted hair shone
Seductively in the quintessential Tim Burton doom lighting.
Or if it took the close-up of her delicate hands
Pounding human flesh into pies for eager customers
To turn my head.
I know what you're thinking
But sexuality isn't black nor white,
And it took Helena's Yvie Oddily curv-ed bodily
Movements to make me realise
This war paint,
Engraved in my brain would have to prepare
For a second coat.
Rainbow stripes.
With glitter.

Beat.

I went to Black Pride,
Found out I could fit there.

11

This woman,

A Glamazonian woman,

She took my hand between hers

And pulled me into the centre of my world.

A new world, yes.

Melanin seeped into my veins

As we all became one being.

One entity.

One community

Within hundreds of others.

Whilst being Black.

As well as.

Because of.

And.

And!

When I think about this world now

I see more... colour.

Black and white, brown and baby blue and orange

and yellow, red, purple, sky blue, pink

And no, I'm not listing the colours of Joseph's

dreamcoat,

Although I wear these colours like a dream.

A dream that allows me to be Black and.

Beautiful.

Intelligent.

Strong.

True.

To myself.

I think that's the most important part of the

assignment, right?

How can we write about the world if we're living a lie?

How can I inject 'and' as a means of demystifying

A world I don't own?

A world I don't actually live in?

Beat.

My world crosses boundaries

Beyond the binary

Existence, filled with electrifying people.

Black people.

Queer people.

Black and Queer.

Black and true.

With glitter, of course.

Body Count
by Nathan Beadle-Towle

Stance David, choosing a Muslim boyfriend and then
bitching about being hidden away is not 'helpless'.
Hysterically refusing to eat because I can't tell
Amira I'm shagging a man on the side is not helpless. You do not get to use that word with me.

Every single night, after we fuck, I lie here trying to
cling to the feel of your sheets, the sound of your
breathing, the hum of your fucking fridge, anything
but the featureless walls of that bombed-out market. Anything but the terror and desperation in their
eyes as my squad breaks cover and runs towards
me, their only chance of survival, sitting on the
mounted gun of that stalled Humvee, hands wring-
ing on the grip of the useless .50 calibre as I fail to
I.D. the insurgents through the mass of hajis trying
to save their fucking goats.

Night after night I watch my men mowed down.
One after the other, after the other. And all I do is
try to meet their eyes as they writhe in the dirt,
because I kid myself that somehow being there with
them at the end makes a difference. Knowing that
any one of Tom and Stevie and Jon-Jon would have
massacred those brown-skinned women and chil-
dren to save me while I did nothing. *That* is helpless.
And as their blood pours out onto the hot, bleak

earth, and their pupils dilate and fix, my brothers
know helpless. It's the last thing they know. You?
You can leave any time. You want some proud fag
to hold your hand while you parade around town?
Go off and find one. The world – your world – is full
of them. But think about this while you're kissing in
the street: I sat in that turret in the blaze of the sun
watching them die twenty feet away from me just
waiting for my turn. Knowing some unseen sniper
was going to shoot me right in the face, zero, *zero*
doubt in my mind that I was about to die, and I
didn't think for one second about the wife you envy
so much. Not a single moment for Amira or the kids.
My own kids. I thought about you, David, and how
you felt inside me, and that I was never going to see
you again.

Born a Homosexual
by Henri Jeremy Leigh

Theo   What do you mean, I'm not allowed in? This is a gay
bar, isn't it? For GAY MEN.

Pause.

I AM a Gay Man. *(Mocking)* A Homosexual Male.

Pause.

Yeah, of course I look different. Thanks for noticing.
It's called 'being an individual'.

Are you asking anyone else for I.D.? Fuck I.D.! I've
had enough of having to tell total strangers my life
story just to prove that I'm human! I am who I say I
am, not a piece of meat or a plastic doll that you
can pull off the top shelf and fuck with. I am not
your fucking fetish!

Mind MY language?! You were the one calling me a
fucking tranny five minutes ago!

You see this? *(Grabbing packer)*

Is this real-enough dick for you? Huh? Do you want
me to whip it out? Like a 'real' man, drunk and taking a piss and celebrated by the rest of the lads?

Imitating a football chant.

He's got 'is dick out! He's got 'is dick out!

Rub it, drip it, shake it out! He's got 'is dick out!

Newsflash darlin'! Not all men have a dick. Whether you see it or not, 1% of your clubbers are intersex and therefore –

What do you mean, 'What does intersex mean?', how did you get this job if you don't even know the basic terminologies for the community that you're *supposed* to be keeping safe?

Karen, can I see your manager?

Oi! Yes, you! You're the manager, right?

Yeah, well, why can't I come in?

Oh, come on! That bear has bigger boobs than me! You're delusional, mate, your head is in the clouds! I'm not a *spicy* straight just because I have a boy-friend! No straight woman takes testosterone! I take it in the arse every morning. And I take on wankers like you every fucking day. I am a *proper* man. I am not some Doctor Who villain, trying to take over the Universe and harvest bodies; This is not *The Curse Of Peladon*. I am not evil and, despite all this bullshit, I am not hateful. *(Mimics Alpha Centauri's shrill, piping voice)* 'I bring peace. I bring love. I am Alpha Centauri.'

Pause.

What's gayer than getting turned away for being a contradiction? Growing up excluded, unwanted... Like damaged goods. Not being seen as 'one of the boys' while knowing deep down you're not a girl on the inside, despite what people think they can see.

Dancing on your own at the school disco, crying in the corner in the darkness.

Taking refuge in new, fascinating worlds of art and expression only to realise everyone sees your spirit as diseased and your work as demented.

Reduced through oppression and fear to communicating with others who are like you with that side-eye. Us men, us homosexual men, can share whole histories with a glance. In your eyes I can read your shame story, and you recognise the pain and longing behind mine. You see? We're not such different men. Just like you, I too was born a homosexual.

Let's talk together, over a drink; tonight, in your club. I am one of you. You are one of me. We are a community.

Now, shake my hand, my friend.

And let me in.

Bridge of Sighs
by Daniel Grimston

*CHARLIE and Seb stand under the Bridge of Sighs in Oxford.
It's the end of the night and the clubs have closed. Shadows
mostly, but faint yellow light from a streetlamp gilds the
dark. They've just had a fight.*

Charlie These bruises... *(He looks at his hand)* I'm not sorry.

Seb turns to go.

> We have to talk, Seb, or things are just going to get
> worse.

Seb turns back.

> Tonight, when your hand landed on my leg in
> 'Spoons for the thousandth time, something shifted
> in my mind. Why do we have to dismiss this? Every-
> one has seen us dancing – the way your hand sits so
> naturally in the small of my back. They've all made
> their assumptions. And... I don't want them to be
> wrong, Seb.
>
> Do you?
>
> If they've already worked out what we're failing to
> hide, then why bother to hide it? Even if we wanted
> to, these bruises mean that we can't. As long as

they're there we'll be reminded of how much we mean to each other every time we look in the mirror.

He looks at Seb.

I panicked – you were about to leave in the cab with that girl and – god, that's just not you. You know it's not you. That's why you panicked too. Fighting instead of…

Seb shifts uncomfortably.

Come on! I'm bored of going home alone, knowing you're a few miles away, having meaningless sex you don't even enjoy. I'm bored of calling you in the morning to hear you say how much you missed me, what a mistake it was. I'm bored of your silence when I ask you why you still do it when we both know how much it makes your skin crawl. I am no longer satisfied with this *Brideshead* shit – dancing around ourselves, pretending that we don't want to tear each other's clothes off. I can't wait anymore, Seb, and after tonight – I won't. Not even for you.

Let's go. Right now – Tangier, Ibiza, Paris – the next county – even fucking Cambridge. Find something new, leave behind these pretenses.

Love each other.

I love you.

I've been scared of those words but it feels like
they're the only ones that will get through to you.
And get me through this. I don't ever want to hurt
you again.

Charlie holds out his hand.

I just want the truth.

Camp With Intent
by Alexander Hopwood

VINCE, TV producer, 20s.

Vince   Okay – cut. Mark… You're still not getting it. For this test, we need more oomph. This is reality TV – there is no time for subtlety. The average human now has an attention span of eight seconds. I'm greedy, I want all those eight seconds. I don't want my viewers checking their TikTok or whatever else is trending. 'Obvious' is how we make money here. And that's how you'll make money.

I think it was Dolly Parton that said, 'Find out who you are. Then do it on purpose.' You see it a lot on Pinterest boards, Facebook, inspirational quote signs in retail park garden centres. People lap it up but they don't really *get it.* They think it's Oprah and Deepak going on about being yourself. But Oprah and Deepak are wrong. What Dolly is actually saying is: work out who your character is. Are you the housewife? The hippie? The hunk? If you want to get out of Locust Ridge you need to nail it down, turn it up to ten and monetise. That's selling. And I want to see and sell you.

Look, I can see you're smart. So – be smart. Play the game. Give us a gimmick! Do you have a cackle? Could you loosen up the wrist? Play up the camp thing and we could be onto something very lucrative here. I know, I know – gay people come in all shapes and sizes, every colour of the fucking rainbow. But the rainbow is too Technicolor. I wish we could bring you through with all the beautiful nuance of a watercolour, but 'they' – the straights, the 94% – won't get it. Vicky at home doesn't get the intricacies of LGBTQ representation. But Vicky will buy your calendar. Vicky will buy your book. Go up the chain and Vicky's basically gonna buy you a house. 'Cause Vicky likes camp. She's not threatened. Mike down the pub isn't threatened. The kind of camp they want is sexless. You have to make them forget that your sex does not result in the sanctified creation of another blessed life. Nothing turns them off faster than thinking about you getting dicked in the arse by another guy. No one wants to shag Rylan, but they would if they saw his bank balance. Camp is innocent and camp pays.

I do it every day. I mince in and give it the 'babe' this and the 'doll' that. I'm just the harmless dizzy queer. Does it make me feel gross? Absolutely. Do I wish I didn't have to deliver everything palatably high pitched? Of course. Am I sick to fucking death of the 'hunties' and the 'werk, girls' and the 'yas kweens'? Entirely. They can't, they won't, see me any other way. But the joke is mine. Now I'm a producer on one of the most watched shows on British

TV. And one day, this will be my show. And then my network. And I will stop being the office Jonathan Van Ness and I will remove the sugar and serve it like it is. But to get there, we all have to play the game. If you want to take the edge off until that point… there's ways. Don't you want to be rich? Don't you want that power? I want you to be on TV. But you have to trust the system.

So. What do you think? Are you gonna give it a go?

Smart choice. I'm going to roll camera. Okay, Mark, straight down the barrel. Tell us a bit about yourself.

Chem Culture
by Max Percy

JEREMY, playing age 19-26. Any ethnicity.

Jeremy I think I got raped. Yes I did. I was drunk in his bed
after a laugh and he said he liked me. Three Gs
later, an hour in between, and vapour on my breath
tells me I'm close to death. So he watches and he
waits while I pretend to masturbate. Then the shit
in my crack he fucks while I hack the drip drip drip
in the back of my nose. Row after row after row
after row. Too much meth makes me easy but a
cock ring ain't a substitute for marriage. Ding ding
ding ding ding ding ding ding. Then bells of a great
clock tower, ticking my life away every quarter of an
hour. Like a barnacle against a rock I dislodge myself
from his cock. I don't want to be a statistic. My feet
think in numerals as they one two one two, right
left right – I left my tobacco in his room, fuck. Leave
it. One sock two sock, D, E, F thirty-seven, twenty-
four. What's the code to this fucking door? Taxi. Hi.
Yes, I am Jeremy. SE14 5NB.

I feel lonely. Directionless, motionless with no journey. It wasn't my fault. He must have misunder-
stood. I said I felt sleepy – but I didn't think that he
would. Not my fault, but I shouldn't have gone to
his. Men can't get raped. That's what my friend

said. But if the proof is in the pudding, my pudding is –

He reaches behind himself then looks at his fingers.

Sharp scratch. Just like that. A blood pact. I am never going to do that again. I don't even need to read the assembly instructions for these test kits anymore. You always think, 'Don't you come up, you cheeky second spot son-of-a-bitch!' I hope that the blue pill I took ten minutes before will save me a red dot now. Come on, please don't show. I can't have this, I can't. My mum will kill me. I'll sleep early, be healthy and practise safe sex. I'll use my Nutribullet and drink kale and chia seed smoothies while I'm on the phone – 'Bye grandma. Bye grandpa. I love you!' See! I can quit any time. I had a bad couple of days. I just needed to get that one out of my system. I really can stop anytime I want.

But I've had a shit week and I'm in my bedroom. I wait on my virtual street corner. Someone take my youth away? Someone enjoy it today. Fun tonight? NSA for DNA. Discreet, masc, tight. Haven't we spoken before? Yeah, you asked me for sex. I think… I think I said yes.

Coming Out as a Gay (Basher)
by Sam Purkis

KAI, dishevelled and, well, looks like he's just finished
fucking. Post nut clarity/cloudiness has begun to set in...

Kai   Fuck. Okay. Fuck. Okay. What was that? What did
we just do? What did you just do to me? I'll put
your head through the fucking window, yeah.
Watch. I'll take my little strip of silver and I'll wet
you, I'll skin a bit of you, what bit shall I do, hmm?
Your chest? Your thighs? Your face? I'm not – I'm
fucking not. How many times have I said? You
should know me. I'm not fucking one of them. I
don't, you know. Men. I don't. We're mates. That's
it. I was at your fifth birthday, you got a...

I gave you your first blunt, remember? We took
your brother's scratched-up moped when he left it
outside his girl's house cos he was being a cunt; we
bunned it on the beach and you said 'I can hear the
stars' or some shit, and that we'd never let anything
come between us. You'll tell no one. Nothing.
Nothing happened. Promise. It was nothing. You're
nothing. I wouldn't even spit on you. Don't come
near me. Barely anything happened anyway.

I hate you for making me see you. I just noticed you,
that's all it was, I just noticed you. That was it. I
couldn't think about anything else. Sarah. Sarah and

I felt like a distant memory, I can't recall a conversation I've had with her and I know that sounds shit, it's not a woman thing or anything like that, my mum would chin-check me for that. I've been like a knock off radio my whole life, the err, fuzzy sound erm frequency reaching nothing, and hearing only the faintest sound of crackles of loneliness but you – you tuned in and I could hear everything, music lived inside my chest, food was orgasmic – even water tasted like that posh lemonade, you know the one you get in the can with the tin foil hat, little Tory Fanta. I never listened to so much Bowie and Prince – even the fucking 'artist formerly known as' years. You smell like sun cream and raspberries. All the time; I think I can smell it in the winter too. I thought I'd devour you, you were so delicious, but I realise you've devoured me. You've taken your feelings, urges and put them in me, infected me. Injected me. You're a brother to me not a lov–

To be honest most of my feelings for you aren't this wet flowery bollocks. They're primal, animal, filthy and raw. I feel so powerful when we are together. I've always been scared I might break Sarah when we fuck but with you, fuck – we really fuck, I just push and push and I feel like a god, like Odin and Thor are going to come crashing through the Bifrost as I cum with an invite to dine in Valhalla. My cock like a warhammer, rigid, curved and deadly.

I need you to understand that I don't want to do this, I've been in agony over it, it really hurts, you know? I have to. For me and maybe even for you. Nah, probably just me. I'm not gonna get to fuck you again, smell you, kiss you, see you or be seen ever again. It's me who's alone after this, but this can't ruin everything. I want this to feel normal but I don't know, how can I feel that this is normal when I see people being slaughtered for it? Outcast because of it, beaten, raped, spat at. If that's what normal is, well, then what's the fucking point?

I love you. I love you. I see you. That's why you've got to go. Goodbye Danny. I love you.

Confession
by Rebecca Downing

*Inside St Mary's, a Roman Catholic church affiliated with
HAYLEY's school, in her local parish.*

*HAYLEY watches fellow pupil Nkem walk over to light a
candle and wanders aimlessly. She sees the door to a
confessional booth ajar, goes in and sits down, tired. She
peers through the grill to ascertain whether anyone is on the
other side, but can't quite tell. After a while she begins to
talk quietly.*

Hayley I'm actually just here with a friend but I thought,
you know, when in Rome. Haha.

There is no response.

To be honest this place always gives me the creeps
a bit.

Beat.

Nice statues. I like the one of Jesus with his top off.
Ripped.

Beat.

Figure he'd be your type too, like.

Beat.

Bit on the mature side I suppose...
Sorry.
That was well rude.
I know you're not all... you know.

Beat.

> D'you reckon a lot of you are though? Not paedos, I
> mean, just... you know. *Into...* grown up Jesus.

Beat.

> As opposed to 'in the manger' Jesus. Just Jesus like,
> on the cross. Station Three's probably the best look.
> Bit less kinky, isn't it.

No answer.

> Shouldn't have said some of that stuff, should I?
> Shit.
> Whoops.
> Don't send me away, sorry. I'm not like a *heathen* or
> anything, I'm just a bit...

Beat.

> Do you ever get lonely?
> You must do, hey?
> Or do a bunch of you lot live together? Or maybe
> that's nuns...
> Where do you live?

Hayley is met with silence.

> Yeah, I guess that's not how this works.

Beat.

> You know I won't lie to you, I might be a bit of a
> heathen. Obviously. I mean you'd know anyway,
> right? Or is that God?

I wouldn't know where to start. Bit of a long list, to be honest.

I've been a very naughty girl.

Beat

Didn't mean that – Sometimes my mouth just runs off somewhere and I'm spouting utter sh... Ahhh, Hayley. Shut up, right? God just – you just –

Father, I think I'm gay.

Long pause as Hayley processes what she's just said.

And that's not a shit-spouting – sorry... thing. But I think I'm *actually* gay, like as in not just in a sexy 'think-about-it-sometimes-if-a-boy's-there' kind of gay but like really, fully, 'I want to wear Doc Martens' kind of gay.

Beat.

But I mean, am I? I mean I've been having *sex* for like a year now and maybe I'm just bored of it or something...

Right. Yeah, that is another one. Yeah, sorry – I told you there'd be a list so you can't say I didn't warn you.

I just...

I actually don't even know why I'm telling you this but –

I just need –

To talk to someone.

Like, anyone.

Beat. Hayley is beginning to get upset.

Like *God*. Like I just need to talk to God right now. Even if he hates me. Even if he wants to – I don't know, smite me down or something.

I'm not sad, I don't know why I'm crying, I'm just – Fuck! I mean flip. Oh god, what's the point? We're past it now.

Beat

I'm sorry. I don't know why I'm sorry. I shouldn't be sorry. I just don't understand. I don't understand why it's so bad.

And none of the other shitty stuff I've done I feel bad about but *this* is like...

Like I feel *SO* bad. *So* bad. What the fuck is that?

Like, is it wrong?

Is it though? Why?

I'm not... I'm not hurting anyone. I just want someone to love me, like, I don't understand why that's so bad.

I don't get it. People are going to hate me when they find out, like really hate me. Like my mum, oh my God. She's not going to...

I've slept with so many boys and she doesn't give a flying fuck, but like I genuinely think she'd rather I got pregnant than this.

I just don't know what to do. And I don't have anyone to talk to. And I need that, I need someone to help me, I need you to help me, please.

Even if you can't, just say you can, just for like...
a minute.

I just need a minute.

Beat

Father?

No answer.

Copycat
by Rory Howes

George   Yep. Sure. That's it, you've got it. Another gold star for James! I came out to my friends because I wanted to copy you. God forbid I should do anything for myself that *isn't* about you, right?

You know, I actually hoped it *was* a phase? I bet you don't even know what that feels like, since you're so perfect and well-adjusted, like, 'Oh, I'm just this cool guy who likes sports and slags off women and just *happens* to be gay.' Mate, you *suck* at being gay. You don't even watch *Queer Eye*. *Dad* watches *Queer Eye*, and he still thinks Jeremy Clarkson should be Prime Minister.

But I was so excited to think that if I was straight maybe I'd have *one* thing you wouldn't have. *One* little thing you couldn't take from me. But nope. Guess I'm just copying you again, just your annoying little brother who follows you around everywhere you go, and ruins your fun, and upsets your friends because no one wants to play with a stupid kid like me. Well, I'm sorry to stamp on your massive sodding ego, James, but this actually isn't about you. It's mine, and it's not going away, and I don't want it to! And you can't touch it, because... because, gurl, I'm here, I'm queer and I'm ready to fuckin' WERK. YASS. KWEEN.

Snatched.

And I'm not apologising for not telling you. You know how I feel about you. You're smarter than me, you're funnier than me. You can actually catch a ball. And you've always, always known who you are. Like you're the Beyoncé, and I'm the Michelle. But you know what? Michelle is *really* talented. Her first album won a MOBO award, and she's making some excellent strides in the world of Broadway musical theatre!

The only thing you were never good at was making me feel like I was worthy of being your brother. And that's actually totally fine, you know, because I don't need your approval. I'm going out there, and for once people are gonna look at me. And when they ask who I am, I'm gonna tell them I'm Michelle fucking Williams, bitch, and I'm my own damn person.

And I bet you don't even know who Michelle Williams is. I'm right, aren't I? Jesus. How have I been giving you so much *credit?!*

Well now it's your turn. I'm done living in your shadow. From now on, I'm walking in front.

In six-inch goddamn heels.

Do You Remember?
by Mical Nelken

Kia   Sorry, stop. Fuck, this was a mistake. You're so beautiful, I can't share your skin with anyone else. Get off her!

Mate, I know. I know I set you both up, I know I just barged in. Please, just take your pants and leave us, okay?

I'm sorry, my light. I fucked up. I'm fucked up. I honestly can't tell you what I was thinking. Maybe I wanted to see if I was over you. Maybe I wanted to see what it looked like to have sex with you. Maybe I wanted to test you – see what it was you were trying to tell me when you told me you were bi.

All I know now is I want you. For myself, I mean. I want to count the curls of your hair around my fingertips, I want to smell the warmth of your neck, I want to hear you breathing softly at night.

If we'd had the words – the imagination – to contemplate love between two women as obvious, as shining, as ours, would it have been easier? We've always been lovers, somehow. At least to me you've always been mine.

Or would it have been harder? Is it the tension in our desire that keeps it alive, not quite knowing how to move, but feeling the embers under our skins burst into flames when we brush hands? Is this what makes us irreplaceable? Why we chase after each other, never daring to get close enough to conclude the chase?

Maybe I shouldn't sleep with you tonight, however much I crave you. But, please, Goddess, don't sleep with him.

Familiar Taste
by Lantian Chen

Jason Liang   Babe! Hurry the fuck up! (*Posing sexy on bed*)
And give that dick a nice wash 'cause I am gonna
ride you all night! Where's the lube? In your
nightstand?

*Finds something unexpected: an enormous dildo. Elliot
comes in.*

>Is this yours?
>Wow.
>It's like the size of a... (*comparing it to his arm*)
>So you're into fisting now? Well, this is news to me
>'cause I remember you telling me your ass was too
>tight for my dick...
>Hmm. Asian dick versus elephant dildo.
>Should I be flattered?

*Tries to stuff it into his mouth – choking, he sort of manages
to fuck his mouth.*

>That's a familiar taste. Delicious, as always. *(Beat)*
>Why didn't you let me fuck you? I prefer to be top, I
>told you. I only bottomed for you because...
>
>No, I didn't like it. No, no, no. I didn't! No.
>
>I did it because I love you, Elliot Dallen. (*Beat*) But
>do you love me?
>
>In what way? (*Beat.*) Different from those masc-for-

masc white guys on Grindr who only see Asian boys as fuckable foot slaves? Any way different from your best buddies on the crew team who gang up on Tinder and lure girls for a threesome, foursome, fivesome? Any way different from treating me as just a hole?

Don't bullshit me, Elliot. You. Like. Getting. Fucked. You LOVE getting fucked. Just not by me.

I know I'm not perfect. I'm awkward and geeky and shy and I'm scared to death at what my mom will do when she finds out about us. I'm not like your thousands of buff Instagram followers. But I love you, Lio. Everything about you, I love. I love that you're so passionate about history that you raise questions in class our Harvard professor can't handle – I love that you slept at the hospital for a week and made me incredible dishes during my fever that taught me to love vegetables, I love that you called your puppy Napoleon.

And I do love feeling you inside of me. When you kiss my nipples and then ruthlessly pump me. I love your muscular arms that row those heavy oars every morning at 6 a.m. and wrap around my neck while you're fucking me till I can't breathe. I love those blue eyes. I love your blond hair. I love your pale white feet. I love that pink hole.

And I'd love you to finally let me in.

Fanx for Nuffin' Dave
by Aoife Smyth

Gal   Mum barges past with an attitude laid on so thick
you see the green stink marks oozin off her
She barricades the stairs in front of me
Looks me dead in the eye
And presses
I found your shoebox last night
Shit
From behind her back she pulls my beloved shoe-
box
Bursting to the brim with little glossy paper islands
Ripped and clipped, tucked under my bed for safe
keeping
Ain't exactly contraband
But in this house, when your brother's the editor of
ID mag and a raging homosexual
This means two things
One, you get free copies of any fash magazine ya
want and ample opportunities to rip out pictures of
gorgeous girls I long to be... with
And two
Your mum's petrified you'll turn out the same way.
Her eyes are burning on my cheeks
I assess the situation – with a mum like mine I've
become a world class liar, see, Tracey Beaker ain't
got shit on me –
Hello? I found that shoebox what's it doing under
your bed
It's for a school project
What project?
Art project
You never do homework

I was passionate about this one
What, 'bout naked ladies?
My chest feels like it's dissolving
They're not naked, Mum
Are you getting these filthy fings from your bruvva?
If they were for school why were they under your
bed?
And before I can answer
Dave winds up the stairs
Dave
Fucking Dave
No brand trainers Dave
Shouts off the scaffolding with his builder mates at
us holding hands beer in his hand Dave
Mum's new side piece, Dave
He gives me this look as if he knows what's coming
A triangle has formed on the top of the stairs
Dave don't get involved
What's going on here then?
Dave she said don't get involved
She?
We can throw them away then can we?
No! Shut up Dave
She?
Oh no it's happening
She?
Oh god here we go
Who's she the cat's mother?
If you're the cat's mother then call me pussy mum
because you are what you fucking eat

Without even thinking she just raises her hand
bound in fake gold jewellery and slaps me, right
round the chops

Dave sniggers
What the fuck are you laughing at Dave?
And I nut him
Doubly as hard
Prick

A stunned silence sweeps the stairwell
Blood trickles down his nose
Calmly
I glide into the bathroom
Chuck him a tampon, tell him to shove it up his
schnoz
Gather my femme fatales
And fuck off out of there

Never saw Dave again
After that.
After that
Never had to hide my clippings
Or anything,
Nice one
Cheers
Dave

Fearless
by Darius Shu

Max   Why was I in a sleazy sweaty gentlemen's club,
Alex? To tell you the truth... I wanted to be. For
years I've tried to be the son my dad has wanted
me to be. The straight guy who thinks about football 24/7 and loves having endless discussions about
the size of a girl's boobs. So, when my uncle took
me there, to make me forget you and open me up
to the world of women – to make me a man – I was
all in. Anything that might stop me thinking about
you. Talking about you. Wanting you. I wanted to
erase every memory of you that makes me smile...
the feeling in my stomach every time you devastate
me with one of those sweet hellos, the heat from
your body whenever we sit next to each other in
chemistry class... All of it. I wanted to escape your
beautiful, shy, but fearless, eyes. I wanted – needed
– to be free of you.

But when the stripper showed me her breasts, all I
could think of was your chest calling out for me to
rest my head there. As she whipped me with her
sexy long hair, I found myself longing to run my
hands through your curly hair. While she whispered
in my ear all I could hear was your soft sexy raspy
morning voice murmuring my name. With this
amazon dancing around me, I was back in that hot
summer night, drunk in the garden with you, lying

there in our boxers... dancing together, sharing my earbuds, singing along to the lyrics of all your favourite songs.

I'm actually genuinely glad I went to that club. I'm grateful to that gorgeous girl who worked so hard and failed. And even to my uncle and dad, 'cause thanks to them I now know one thing for certain – that I only feel alive when I'm next to you. And how deeply I am in love with you. And that where I belong is with you, kissing every kiss we've both been waiting for all our lives.

That loving you has made me into a man.

A man like you.

Fearless.

Finding AJ
by Alex Theo

River Most people I know, know someone they lost to cancer. Bruv, I even lost my fish to cancer. Can you fucking believe that? My Nemo. Nah not the film Nemo, my Nemo was Nemo before famous Nemo came along. Famous Nemo needed to find Dory, my Nemo never needed anything other than some cod liver oil, I guess. God rest his soul.

When I lost Nemo, I decided it was time to move on and meet another man: AJ. Never thought I'd have a man, just like I never thought I'd be gay, yet here we are. AJ asked me how he looked… Bald. He looked like a dad with seven kids and a heavy mortgage he's struggling to handle, so that's exactly what I said… He was cracking up.

AJ has cancer, Non-Hodgkin's lymphoma, few months in seeing him he ended up getting cancer, great start. Basically me and AJ call it the X-Men Disease, so technically my man's Professor Xavier, but don't worry, this time I am making sure he is taking his cod liver oil.

AJ. What does dying feel like? 'Well, River' – yeah, my name's River – still holding my hand, 'the thought of being able to sleep for eternity is rather exciting.' He was being deadly serious; you know how deep of a sleeper he is? Listen, World War 3 can happen just outside our door and he'd sleep through it. Me? I'm a light sleeper, any noise I'm like a fox, BAM, who at my door? That's what I love about us, the balance of us, you know? Like, he'd be a vegetarian and I'd be a meat eater; to compromise I'd make him a chicken curry and pretend it's this special tofu I got from M&S. 'This proper taste like chicken! I know, right?'

He took my head and told me to look into his eyes. (He always did stuff as if he knew what I was thinking, told you my man is Professor Xavier.) 'Promise me something,' he said. He said it again, but the pressure from his hands on my neck grew tighter... I said, if it's to not fuck again, I can't be doing that. Sorry, but no, don't judge me, he can ask me to do anything but that. Listen, I'd sit by his grave singing SIA songs all day, but nah, I can't not have sex, sorry. 'No,' he said. 'Make an effort with my mum.' AJ's mum knows about us, but just doesn't want to know, if that makes sense. I reckon if *The Purge* was real, she'd definitely come after me. 'Trust me, if there's anyone that can help her, you know, after I'm gone, it'll be you. Just try to be there for her, no matter how much she pushes you away. Also, I need you to sing a song for me when you visit my grave, every single time, without a fail. Our song.

'Take Me Home' – John Denver.'

Pause.

Grief. I just wasn't ready for it… A bit like bottom-ing.

Okay, so this is the bit in the story where you're thinking, oh god, did he die?

Pause.

Now, as I stand over your grave, for once I'm the top!

You have a beautiful family, even though I watched from afar, for obvious reasons. I just didn't want your mum, you know, having any other stress than just grieving over her only son.

Now, as I'm staring down at your grave, I'm prepar-ing to sing this fucking song…

River looks around, he notices a family beside him at another grave.

Hi, condolences to you all –

He awkwardly looks back at AJ's grave, takes a deep breath and begins to sing the opening lines of 'Take Me Home' by John Denver.

I then hear a leaf crack behind me. Someone else is singing the song. I turn round. It's your mum.

She comes closer to me whilst singing it.

She holds my hand. Carries on singing, we both sing together.

I slowly reach around and embrace her. She smells like you, you know.

I love you, man. I will always. Always. For eternity.

I guess this was my proper goodbye.

You're finally home now.

Fizzy
by Paul Bradshaw

Alex   I fancy everyone. I'll meet someone and if there's a spark, which there usually is, I'll roll with it. I've always been the same. From the age of 8 or 9 I've had that same, like, fizzy feeling around girls or boys. Obviously, at that age you don't have a fucking clue what's going on, but it's definitely a fizzy feeling though, right? Like, butterflies or whatever?

I've never actually been on a date with a guy. I've known Leon for years and we've always had this crazy mad chemistry, but it's never worked out. I've always had a girlfriend or... or he's been loved up. Ships in the night. But we're both single now so I thought 'fuck it', let's go on a date. We've hung out loads before but because this a more... romantic vibe I'm definitely feeling a bit... *(noticing Leon)* Oh, shit!

Leon approaches – Alex waves awkwardly.

He looks fit. He's wearing an oversized vintage shirt and tight Levi's shorts. Sunglasses on, his trademark quiff in his hair, which never seems to budge when the wind picks up...

We're flirting our way down the Southbank, stealthily dodging tourists, sipping our iced lattes.

We're laughing, I'm talking, he's listening – like, really listening. You know that way people listen where they make you feel like you are the only person that matters? Like that. He's special.

(Laughs madly) Was that a joke? It wasn't? Fuck. I'm sweating. Am I moving my hands too much? Was he listening intently or was he just bored as fuck? I shouldn't have come. What is he...?

He's reaching up and putting his arm around me. Is he trying to make me relaxed? Or is it to shut me up? My fizzing is now a buzz all over my body. I feel like a teenager again. My breath is getting high in my chest. Right, Alex, keep calm. Deep breaths, act cool. Keep. Your. Cool.

I slowly turn to look at him. He's smiling. He starts to lean in – Is he? Yeah, he's going for it, and I'm letting him. God. We're kissing. Right outside the Tate fucking Modern.

It's a nice kiss, awkward at first, a bit... exposing. It's odd, I thought it might have felt wrong... but it doesn't. It feels... good, normal. It's nice. Fizzy.

For You
by Ashen Gupta

Kamala (Kam) 'Latte please, and for you? ...Latte and a hot
chocolate please.'

I'm in an independent coffee shop for what feels
like the first time in years. This city is new to me
and, to an extent, so are you, sitting opposite,
smiling apologetically, and I'm having a hard time
figuring out why.

My last memory of you is covered in spots and
shame and a letter that never had a reply.

Today I'm visiting Nottingham on my national grand
tour of old schoolmates in their rundown uni halls.

'How have you been? I can't believe it's been two
years since we saw each other.'

You break out into a grin and I slurp down nostalgia
with my coffee. I hate caffeine, but not being able
to go to university meant that, alongside not getting
a degree, I can't be a shabby teen who drinks hot
chocolate instead of tea.

Laughs.

'Do you remember my thirteenth birthday party?
It's still to this day the worst party I have ever
thrown – no, it was awful! You were the only one

out of fifteen people to show up!'

I remember that party like it was yesterday. It re-
plays in my mind, so I tell you how I was only allowed to invite fifteen mates, when the truth was I only
ever wanted you to stay.
I say how relieved I was that at quarter past eight
you finally turned up at my doorstep, prepped with
a pillow and a Schweppes lemonade.
The *Sherlock* marathon came first, then *Hot Fuzz*,
then *The World's End* and before it was midnight
we had committed to memory every scene of *The
Bee Movie*. One a.m. brought us popcorn and Nutel-
la and leftover pakoras and an embrace that lasted
an eternity. A kiss shared during the final moments
of *Toy Story 3* ended abruptly when footsteps came
thudding downstairs and a voice squinting in dim TV
light tells us it's late and swears under their breath.
Our cosy den became chillier then for reasons I
couldn't comprehend.
Was it fear?
You were always so brave.
Or the icy shock of a shameful act?
I never plucked up the courage to ask.

I can't ask now.

You fill me in on the details of your life. Where
you've been, what you've seen. Your trip to Iceland
sounds like a dream. Your string of boyfriends, all

with names beginning with A, and they blur into one as I listen to your melodic voice drone on.

I nod.

Drink coffee.

Smile.

Fuck Me
by Michaela Mackenzie

Alex   FUCK! Fuck fuck fuck.

Sorry.

You weren't meant to hear that. You're just really attractive. I keep almost telling you – Shit.

I've just done it again.

You're tangling up my brain and I can't filter my words right now cos you're really infuriatingly mesmerising –

You're frustrating me.

Do you know that's a real emotion? When you feel angry at someone for being so beautiful – s'called hanker sore – google it – not hostile though, just irrational anger, saw it on a YouTube video.

I don't know what's happening.

I drank three shots of the Don Julio 1942.

Shouldn't be telling you that.

I wasn't going to but the guy paying for the party made me. He said everyone should know what it tastes like and especially me as a bartender. He said he's effectively paying your salary so he'll deal with it if you disagree. It did go down smooth.

You always put your hand on my shoulder.

I just like physical contact. That's creepy isn't it? Am I being creepy?

But then I can feel you aren't angry with me. No matter what you're saying I can feel your warm comforting hand. And you always call me your

dearest darling. And you say my name.
Please don't stop that. I really like it.
I am creepy.
Shit.
Why can't I stop speaking?
I don't want to have sex with you.
A)   You're my boss so we kinda… well… can't -ish
B)   You have a bit of a reputation, man.
Which is fine. Obviously.
You may sleep around as you wish, good sir. Weird
choice of words there.
But I don't like it when you cheat on people.
None of my business, sorry.
Honestly that kind of ruins you for me.
I wish you didn't have sex. I wish sex weren't a thing
in life. That things never escalated to sex.
That's what's great when you're a child, you get to
fancy someone and you can flirt and fancy each
other but you don't have sex. There's no expecta-
tion. I wish it ended there.

I've never said that to anyone.
Damn your hand on my shoulder.
I shouldn't have told you all this.
I'm gonna get fired aren't I.
No one else drank the Don Julio. He only made me.
Please don't fire anyone else.

Get Woke
by Dior Clarke

Dillz   Look at all of you.
Same faces,
Standing in the same places,
Talking about the same drama on a regular basis.
Fighting and killing your brothers and sisters for a
postcode you will never own because the bludclart
government owns it.
Blind and lost in the smoke you can't see outside
the box, dealing. On the rob
They love it, you're helping them do their job.
AIN'T YOU SEEN THE FUCKING NEWS?
Or do you refuse?
Black people getting hot down, held down, choked
Viruses killing our black arses, get woke.
So sorry that I've made a choice to live my life being
unapologetically me,
Sorry my out there confident 'Batty Man' persona
threatens your big black masculine balls,
Sorry I stepped outside the box
you're still stuck in by choice.
I used to deepen my voice way back in the day
Alter my walk to look less gay,
Tame my dress sense to look less flamboyant,
Fight every day like a bad bwoi so people like you
wouldn't mess with me,
Dance in a boyish way when all I really wanted to do
was wine up my waist,

I used to fuck more gyal than all of you and still could if I wanted to.

My master plan was to keep dating girls, get married and have sex with men on a down-low.

A notion some of you are very familiar with, I know Because I used to fuck some of you scared closet wastemen.

Don't worry I ain't got time to out none of you, it's your life and journey so how about you let me go on my journey in peace.

I ain't scared of you anymore or what anyone thinks of me.

I've actually experienced more drama and trauma on the black gay scene.

Imagine a bunch of 'yous' but gay and even more broken because not only do they have to face the struggles that come with being a black man in society, but because their discriminated community discriminates them,

disowns them,

mentally, physically and emotionally abuses them and in some cases fucking kills them. It's like a pool of broken human beings trying to get one up on each other but deep down all they want is love.

I had to take myself away from that scene like I had to take myself away from you lot.

Finally realised it's not about searching for love and acceptance

It's about giving yourself the love you seek, and

giving the love to others that you want to receive.
Whether you're

gay,

lesbian,

straight,

bisexual,

transgender,

intersex,

non-binary,

queer!

And you know what, If I could wake up straight tomorrow I would wake up gay because I love me gay as fuck!

And I am not your biggest threat nor are other black people. There's a bigger war to be fought and I'm fighting it. And so should you.

Get! Woke!

By the way I'm not really a 'batty man',

I'm more of a 'dicky man' because boy I do love me some dick.

(Blows kiss)

Laters!

Girl Meets Girl
by Tamara Vallarta

Tabatha   I've been writing a movie script.

Girl meets girl.

They'd met once before, years ago. She remembers
Her in her green outfit talking about not being able
to have kids— and now She sees Her in this party
and thinks, 'There she is – the most beautiful woman in the world.' And they talk all evening, and She
starts inviting Her out and suddenly realises, 'Oh my
God, I like Her!'

A LOT. Since... Always.

But she probably can't imagine it going anywhere
because She has always dated guys. Although now
She is realising every time she's liked a girl in a special way without understanding why. So She invites
Her out to tell Her how she feels. And, plot twist: on
her way to the restaurant She learns she's pregnant
from the guy she thought was *the one* but, of
course, definitely wasn't. And anyway He'd always
said he wasn't ready for kids.' So, fine. She decides
to have an abortion, but then He finds out about
the baby, and He is suddenly ready for everything,
and wants a family. But now She is with Her.

Did you know there's false negatives? I had no idea.
I knew I was pregnant on day 5, and I peed on a test
and it said NO. Then my shrink said I was going
manic and gave me new pills. So I became this nau-

seating sleeping-and-peeing moron, blaming every symptom on a mental illness.

For a moment she stops.

And now I don't even want to take the pills because I don't want to hurt it.

She's about to cry but she tries to hold it in.

What an ass, right? I can't keep it. I'd destroy its life.

She looks at her stomach.

I would never be there. I'm always working cuz I'm shit with money — even though I work double shifts. And I just don't have time.

I'm not ready.

And I don't want to take my frustrations out on you — I would, you know. That's what selfish people do. We blame and punish others. I will try to hide it of course, but you will *feel* it. You will see shattered broken pieces and you will make them yours. Insecurity. Fear. Lack of love.

Pause.

Maybe in the film, She can give the baby to Her – the beautiful girl in green. That would be a nicer ending. Or maybe… they could both be moms.

Pause.

Oh, wow... I am sorry. This wasn't the way I rehearsed it, but... Fuck, these days the only time I can get out of bed is when I'm going to see you. And this isn't the hormones or the pills talking. I *like* you. Since the day I saw you in your green dress — and I have to pee cuz I've been peeing since you arrived, but maybe together we can solve this *(she moves her hands around herself)* mess, and maybe... we can rewrite this movie... Together?

Hate You
by Sara Dawood

Nadia   I hate your haircut, it makes you look like such a lesbian. Like every other queer at drag brunch on Saturday. Yeah, it's hot, but it's fucking embarrassing. It's why I didn't take you to meet my friends. Why I recoil every time you go to take my hand or kiss me in public. However much I'm dying to. If you didn't look like that I could take you to meet my mum and pass you off as a work friend or whatever. But I can't do that when you wear those ridiculous slogan tee-shirts that scream *'I am sleeping with your daughter!'* Which I'm glad you are, by the way. It's not even just the clothes or the haircut, though: you wouldn't know how to act. And let's face it, you wouldn't eat her food. If there's one thing she's into, more than casual homophobia, it's force-feeding house guests. And God forbid you remember that she's Iraqi, and she doesn't get the whole gluten-free vegan thing – which, let's face it is some white people shit.

She's not a bad person, she does love me. It's overwhelming how much love there is. More than I know what to do with, more than I deserve. Sometimes I wish she wouldn't love me so much if it meant she could understand. Imagine a love so fierce yet so fragile that you wouldn't dare test it, for fear of it shattering around you.

But you can't. Because your parents took you to your first Pride when you were nine and gave you Judith Butler books at fifteen. They didn't care when we slept together in the same bed under their roof. In the morning your dad brought coffee upstairs for us. He fussed with your wonky curtain rail while my head was in your lap and you twirled a lock of hair around your fingers. You're used to love you can handle.

You'll leave eventually. You couldn't possibly love me like she loves me. The way I love you. But after you dump me, if I still have her, I won't be alone.

Is it so wrong to want a safety net? To keep this secret, if it means Mum continues to love me even after you've stopped?

Do you hate me? As much as you love me? As much she loves me?

As much as I love you?

Heavy
by Rory Howes

Alfie   I mean, yeah. You can call me whatever you want. Except Daddy. Don't call me Daddy please. Haha. I mean you can, if you want. I don't really mind.

Can I just say, you're probably the most attractive person who's ever spoken to me. In my life. So thank you. For messaging me, like.
I mean it though, you're like... really, really fit. Like, Leo, pre-dad bod.

I should just say... I know this is weird, given what we're about to do and all, but I'm gonna keep my shirt on if that's okay. It's nothing, there's nothing weird under there or anything, it's just. I get cold easily. Do you mind?
Sorry.
You've got really nice eyes. Not just eyes, obviously: all of you's nice. Better than nice. Amazing.

Can we move to the bedroom? I feel a bit weird being in your kitchen. Feels like all your friends are gonna jump out from somewhere and like, laugh or something. I'm just kidding. I know, that's stupid. I know. It's just, when you messaged, I thought it might be a joke. I mean, you could have anyone. Seriously. I mean that. Am I like the last one left on the grid?

Haha.

Or is it because I'm...

It's fine. It's okay. I know some people are into that. I mean, I guess I don't really get it, but I don't mind. What I mean is... I'm happy that you messaged me. I think you're really beautiful, and the thing is, people like you don't go for people like me. We don't get along normally, so I have to assume that this is something more for you than it is for me.
– I'm spoiling it. I'm sorry. I want to do this. I'll do whatever you want, I really don't mind. Honestly, if you've got a kink or something. You know what they say about big guys. We're more grateful!

Agh.
Damn it.
I'm sorry, this happens sometimes, I put all the energy into my mouth and then my... thing doesn't do anything. It's not about you, I swear.

Look at you, you're just all pecs and abs and jawline. I mean, your name is Cody, for Christ's sakes. It's obviously not you. You're perfect.

Look, don't even worry about me. Just tell me what you want me to do to you. Whatever you want. Do you want me to eat in front of you, or shake my belly, or wear your clothes? You can call me names. Or feed me, if that's what you're into. I don't mind. Just. Don't take any videos.

And let me stay the night. I'll go first thing tomorrow, I promise. I just want to savour this.

Hey Millie
by Tricia Wey

*STEPH is on the train. She takes her phone out and dials a
number. There's a short silence for a while: voicemail. She
leaves a message.*

Steph Hey Millie, it's Steph Evans! *(Pause)* Obviously.
(Beat) Sorry, that was... weird.

Ummm, I was just calling to say I'm sorry I had to
take off so early; it's just... trains and everything,
you know? Don't have that Uber money, and if I
ever get on a night bus again I think I might actually
throw myself off the top deck. But tonight was fab!

You looked well! Really... healthy. Okay, not
'healthy'; that's a weird choice of adjective, sorry.

Satisfied. I think that's more what I mean.

So, I... came this evening with ulterior motives, I
must admit. And I wanted to have a chance to chat
to you tonight, but it never felt like the right time. I
didn't want to take away from all the excitement of
the evening. And... I chickened out, in all honesty.
This is a lot easier to do when I don't have to look at
your face while I do it.

Fuck, I didn't mean for this to be so... weird.

I just – I *(Takes a deep breath. Quietly)* I want to be with you. *(Laughs slightly)* I want to be with you. I want us to be together.

Can I say that? Is it... too late for me to feel like this? I know George is great; I love him! Honestly, but I see the way you smile around him, and it's not enough. Satisfied... isn't good enough for you. You deserve so much. You deserve the world. And he can never give that to you.

I can.

I know this is selfish of me. I know it's all my fucking fault that we're not together right now anyway. I know we could have had something, something real.

But I was barely ready to come out to myself. To think of myself going home and introducing you to my parents as my girlfriend. Deal with my mum's sad eyes as she asked if I'd *really* thought this through. Try to explain things to my dad. Patiently explain to them that of course this doesn't mean that they'll never be grandparents. To just uproot my whole life like that. I just couldn't. Face it.

But I've been thinking about it so much, and I've realised that none of that matters as long as you're there with me, holding my hand. I just want to make you smile, Millie, every single day. Proper smiles. All-consuming, face-aching smiles that make you feel like your mouth could fall off.

I love you. And I'm pretty sure that you still love me. And I want us to build a life together.

So, just... fuck it!

Fuck the lives we've already built; fuck the explanations we'd have to give; fuck the tiptoeing around like we don't belong together! Fuck it all!

Let's just, I dunno, rent a car and drive up the country and leave everything behind for a bit and just be – us!

Silence. STEPH brings herself back down to earth.

I want that. So bad. But I know that this isn't fair. Because you already have a life and... I can't ask you to give that up just because all of a sudden I'm not scared anymore.

I love you, Millie. And I'm sorry I didn't tell you earlier.

Beat. She looks at her phone, hesitates, presses a button, takes a breath, and lifts it back to her ear.

Hey! Thanks for a great night; sorry I dipped without saying 'bye. The new place is beautiful! I hope you and George like the rug. Can't wait to do it again.

...Ciao, Babes!

She hangs up.

Home on the Ocean
by Ryan Mcveigh

Connor I told Mum about you the other day, about us.
Shhh, it's alright, just listen for a second. I couldn't
keep it a secret anymore. It didn't feel... healthy
anymore. Truth is, it never did. I can't not say who I
really am, Cathal – how I feel about you. The moment she told me my happiness was all she cared
about, sure didn't I start bawling like a wee chile.
We both did. A lot. That's why I wanted you to take
us out here today.

Every time it rained, when we used to come out
here on your dad's dinghy as kids, I almost always
froze my bollocks clean off – and without a jacket,
just so you'd be throwing me over your baggy green
hoodie – the one that smells like that dire Brut after
shave you still wear. When you finally said, 'Haul
onto it,' I was made up. I wore that hoody summer
and winter for months on end every night, even
when I got too big for it. Waking up every morning,
hugged tenderly by a piece of you, carrying me back
to this boat.

You turn to me, pouncing quick like a cheetah, claw-
ing and pulling me in close with your hot grip, noses
touching, staring deeply into my eyes, breathing
heavy on my noticeably chapped lips, and couldn't
care less. In this moment my heart sinks – cue
intense rollercoaster rush racing through me at a

hundred miles an hour, passing all the stop signs. Our bodies connect. Tight. Your hot and heavy breath on my neck, those hungry hands gripping tight on the exterior of my stiff horse-hung cock as you loosen my belt – shoot me up with your euphoric fuck straight into my fresh pulsating veins – yes, more! 'I'm ready for you, Cathal. Do what you want to me,' I'm panting, my heart rate skyrocketing. Ugh yes! Once you're inside me my hands naturally force their way through your bushy, Odysseus-like hair as a thousand sharp, heavy rainfall daggers strike down onto your bare pale back – in that moment I mean something. Wrapping my legs around you like a spider ready to suck in its prey, I pull you in deeper – the immediate headfuck blasts through my brain.

And then best part. The touching, the spooning, fingers entwining... You look at me, thinking I'm sleeping and whisper, 'I love you, Connor O'Shea, and I'm not letting you go – not now, not ever.'

This is the life I want back there, Cathal. The one that hides out here in this boat. Us holding hands wherever we happen to be, happy and in love with someone who wants the same as me and isn't afraid to show it, and not just when it suits them. Each fishing trip is a special voyage. To a place where we're the only people alive and I... I crave that. When I'm with you on this ocean, I'm home. Are you ready to be my home on the land?

Homo Testing
by Sam Cormor

DEE sits on his bed with a parcel in his lap. He focuses on his ear.

Dee   Does this look infected? It feels infected. I went through a whole George Michael phase last year which started with a simple leather and short denim combo and ended with passing out on a public toilet floor after piercing my ear with a corkscrew. Don't get me wrong, I like being back, but I tell you it's a lot harder being George Michael in Gloucester than it is at Garage Night in Vauxhall Fire at 5 a.m. It's nice not having to go to a clinic in person, though, and see the past Daves, Toms, Jordans, The One I Can't Remember and the odd Chloe (weird phase) in the waiting room like a line-up of Who's dunnit this time? At least here I can do it in the comfort of my own, childhood-memory-filled bedroom, only to be judged by the Gruffalo and Shawn Ryder. Is that weird? I think 10-year-old me would be proud. Actually, I think 19-year-old me would be proud. I remember going to a clinic in Hammersmith for the first time and being terrified 'cause I forgot to wash my bumhole and I didn't want the nurse to have a mumsie conversation about wiping properly so I've come a long way.

Beat.

This is not ideal.

I don't think I can do it. It's not that I know what it'll say so there's no point, it's more of the hassle of what happens if it says – if it says positive I just can't be bothered explaining to everyone all the time that I'm actually and unfortunately going to be absolutely fine. That's the problem, I almost feel bad I'll be probably be healthier than the poor people trying to get a scouts' badge for being accepting and queuing to shake my hand like Princess fucking Diana. It's not necessary.

It's boring.

It would be interesting though. Not like in a weird or fetish way but it would actually be quite nice having something real to answer when Auntie Bertel asks what's new at Christmas. It would be a welcome relief for her not to pretend to care about my sloth-paced rise to the top of the TV industry, and I could even throw in a teardrop or two and really milk the whole fighter vibe. She'd love it. She'd bask in it, in the devastation, the personal loss, the trauma, she'd wish she had a story this good to tell at her weekly book club. Although they'd probably throw away the books she'd touched. I'd float around the flat in a kimono and win the Nobel Prize for Literature for my verbatim book on young journeys through diagnosis to acceptance. It would be understated and emotional. 'A real treasure,' *The Guardian* will quote.

Christmas would suck.

Because I won't even be able to get a bit fat 'cause I'd have to fit into the whole InstaPozGang who are so healthy, aren't they. I tell you it's almost a rub in the face from the '80s queens that are now fitter than the straights who were so desperate to get rid of them, and you know, it's gonna be hard to keep up with it. I don't wanna let the side down. I refuse to be the ONLY poz 22-year-old with a beer belly and questionable cocaine habit. I refuse to do a press-up. It's not a good look for for for for for Ter-rance is it? Not exactly a smiling poster boy. Give HIV the finger isn't the same when the finger you're using is to gum MDMA in Metropolis toilets on a Tuesday night with another cute 19-year-old Romanian who found you in the smoking area.

I know, it's the right thing to do – know your status blah blah blah – I don't know why 'cause I've not had sex in 6 months so it's not like I'm a huge risk and just passing it free-nilly like I'm Daryll Rowe. It's the correct thing to do. The right choice. The sensi-ble choice. I can honestly update my profiles and educate myself and the masses and even do a documentary on *Vice*. I'll fight the stigma tooth and nail, get rejected on Grindr, get closer to friends, get abused in the street, take a job at a charity and make a real difference, be exiled from social family events because it's probably too difficult to explain, become a rich influencer......

Opens the parcel.

> ....be just just just really fucking scared, forget to
> take my pill everyday 'cause I'm 85 and my lactose
> intolerant grandkids are coming round and I'm so
> excited I've been baking cheese scones all morning.

The self-test device is inches from his finger.

> See Mum's terrified terrified terrified face —

The prick test clicks.

> Oops.

Looks at the results.

> Oh. Right.

Back to the ear.

> I think this thing is infected you know.

I had to get out
by Charlie S. Smith

Sam   (*Entering, talking to the other room*) I'm just going
to get glasses for the champagne.

Shaken, trying to catch their breath.

I had to get out. At least for a few minutes.
Give me a sec, I have to, like, I don't know, cry?
Shout into a pillow? Punch a wall? How am I
supposed to know, they don't teach you that in
school!?

Pause to calm down a little.

I kept my mouth shut again.
Actually, that's not true. I opened it, and I shut it
right back like a coward.
(*Using a deeper voice/higher voice.*) 'Do you know
the one with the faggot and the beer opener?' he
said.
So I had to get out.
At least this time I don't know how the 'joke' ends.
Avoidance, yay, well done.

Glances back at the room.

Does he know? Do they all know?
I don't think so, I'd have been banned from this
family long ago.

So what?

I do get the 'straight pass', can't I use it as a strength, can I pretend to be an ally? Well, I AM an ally, just not a straight one.

Am I though? An ally I mean, not, you know (*Whispers*) straight.

Can I be true to who I am when I don't speak up? I know I don't NEED to be this or that to defend someone, or to call them out on their shit.

It took everything I had to get up and leave that bloody room.

It's strange, growing up I didn't need to know I wasn't straight to know that hatred was wrong. And yet, that's what they (*nods towards the room*) taught me, hating others, hating myself, for just... Being.

I never got that, it never made any sense.

So why should I be scared of speaking up when nobody knows?

Why can I be an advocate for animal rights and not be considered a panda bear (and let's be honest, I'm just as cute), but not be an activist against homophobia without hearing, 'Why do you care, are you gay?'

Technically, I could get away with a simple 'no': wouldn't be lying, would remain on the will, would still be invited for Christmas.

(*Mutters*) I don't even celebrate Christmas, why do I care?

I wouldn't be true to myself now, would I, if I
pretended not to be me...
I don't want their money, I don't want their love
and acceptance if it's based on a lie... .
So, what do I do now?

Pause, looking towards the other room.

I did get up and leave, that's something right? A
first.
Maybe next time I'll get up and speak.

Maybe next time.

I see You
by Ian Weichardt

Adam Finished!

So, most people will have been crying for the past
24 hours. Me? I've been sculpting my dead friend's
face into one of Tesco's finest organic avocados.
Creative, huh? Where would you be without us
creative types?

I've frozen it. The avocado. Should I have frozen it?
When will I use it? Should I use it? Maybe I could
eat a bit every Christmas in memory of him. But
then I would have to put a knife through his face.
Which doesn't seem particularly memorial-like,
does it?

He used to come over every Christmas with Danny.
That's when things were good. For all of us. Smoked
salmon, avocado and caviar blinis and champagne.
Lots of champagne. For starters. But Nick, that was
his name, Nick, Nicky, Nicola-la-la... always brought
his home-grown avocados. His little babies. Along
with twelve bottles of champagne. Twelve days of
Christmas all rolled into one. Every person got their
own bottle. Dessert as well. Christmas pudding was
rather different for us gays. I'd drift off to sleep on
the couch stroking my food baby, exhausted from
doing all the cooking and wake up with a full face
of glitter felt-tip pen graffiti to find a glistening,

sparkling line of cocaine waiting for me.
MERRY CHRISTMAS BABY! LET'S PARTY!

It was the highlight of the year. For all us boys. The
dress-up box came out. Wigs were on. Dance routines. Karaoke. Drugs and booze flowing. Don't-
Dance-Danny always DJing on the decks. And Danny
and Nicky so in love. Me and Tom, my husband,
never had that spark they had. They ignited each
other and together they lit up the room.
It broke Nicky after Danny left. He didn't know how
to repaint his future.
Me and Nicky kissed once. Only the once. He
shrugged it off the next day but I never forgot that
moment. I felt something. He would always pick me
up and put me on his shoulders and spin me
around.
(*Spinning*) We would sing at the top of our voices,
'Spin me right round baby, right round like a record
baby.'

*Spins faster and faster and falls to the floor in laughter until
sobbing with tears. Looks at and fixates on a point on the
ground nearby.*

I can still see his face when I found him lying there.
Naked. Vulnerable.

He was mine. He was mine to look after. I knew he
wasn't okay, that he had a problem with drugs and I

turned my back on him. I let him rot away, to that.

Looks directly into the face of the avocado.

I see you Nicky. Finally, now I see you. I love you.
Forever and always.

Adam kisses the avocado.

If They Were an Alien
by Laura Crowhurst

Elisha   Her hands, if you have to know! It's her hands. Well,
I mean, *their* hands. Shit, I don't actually know, you
know? She, he, they. Them?

And before you say it, yeah, yeah, they look like a
'boy', which makes them even fitter because it's like
they don't give a shit what you think. They know
themself and it's authentic – it's not for the 'gram,
it's not for likes or shares, it's not an ad.
It's just them.

To be honest, I don't care. They, them, she, he –
whatever.

Christ, if they were an *alien* I'd be in.

Beat.

Who knew you can be both, huh? Beautiful *and*
handsome. With these hands that just caught me.
Like, strong and warm. Not weird and clammy like
Darren's. When they touch me, I dunno, I feel safe
and endangered all at once. I don't feel fat, I don't
feel ugly, I just feel... My mind turns off, all the
voices fade, and I feel quiet and still. I'm exactly
where I'm meant to be. It's bliss – like being held by
a warm, smooth, memory foam statue.

Arrrrgh! It's like they have their own campfire party

going. When I'm near them, there's a glow, I feel their heat on my cheeks.

Takes a breath. Her energy shifts.

Probably easier if they were an alien. We could just zoom off, go whizzing around the galaxy being all happy and stuff instead of all this... expectation.

I wonder if they're vegan?

I keep thinking of their lips.

She has a physical and verbal outburst of excitement.

Sorry. Yeah, it's all hot and stuff but I have no idea what it all means. If it means anything at all. Shit, maybe it means everything, and for now, I like it. I'm happy.

I feel...

She can't find the word.

Maybe that's it...

Beat.

Yeah, that's exactly it.

I *feel*.

Intruder
by Amber Muldoon

KEIRA – late 30s – Irish

Keira   Wait – you're not David – are you new?
Sorry, not wearing my glasses!
I live opposite. Just there – can practically dunk a
hobnob in my Earl Grey from here
Above the big Sainsburys
but I'm a big fan of shopping local so here I am.

I don't normally look like Matt Lucas, by the way. I
panicked.

Keira rubs her head, intrigued.

Wow it feels like... I probably should have just
bought nit cream rather than shaving it a–
So, actually I'll probably have to introduce myself
again – another day.
I don't normally use razors actually because they
give me this horrendous rash.
My other half's a teacher. Teaches autistic kids.
And bless them, one of them must have given them
to her and then – well, they wouldn't have shown
any tell-tale signs. Itching or whatever.
Someone saw one crawling in my hair at work today
– bit embarrassing really but she drives a Punto, so.
I just shaved it off. In the loo – at work – don't know
why.
I should have known; My dad's not a looker.

Maybe I'll have grown a feathered bob by about
June next year for my wedding –
I hope it humbles me.

And the Veet is for the mane down there.
Probably just easier – get rid. Rug and bugs.
My girlfriend likes it childlike anyway.
Like a Cabbage Patch Kid. Or a spiky little Pac-Man
Says she's sick of getting cunt hair in her teeth. So –
Oh, sorry...
Can I just add a Creme Egg?
'How do you eat yours...'

Really? That's actually pretty fucking disgusting.

Oh my god! Oh my god! There's – there's someone
in my flat?!
No – don't look. Fuck. Fuck!
Just block me – stand there! And I can try and –
Yeah.
That's perfect – Thank God you're wide.

Oh Jesus, they're all in black.
Fucking hell.
I'm just gunna try and call my girlfriend – can you
call the police while I call my girlfriend... *(Dialling)* at
the... school?
Oh come on – pick up, pick up. Voicemail – don't
know what I expected.
Should I – Oh hi, darling. It's me.
This is mental but there's someone in our flat – I
can't quite make out what they look like – forgot

my glasses this morning but... Oh, by the way you gave me nits – hysterical – so I'm just here in the corner shop buying Veet because I think they've travelled downward and –
Oh god, I'm so sorry, I don't even know your name... Manuel! ...is calling the police for us. I shouldn't go in there, should I? Manuel, do you sell kitchen utensils? No, that's a stupid idea. I'm awful with... chopsticks –
Hang on – they're coming to the window –
Oh my god – Oh m– Oh my god. I – they've put on your jumper...
and...
Wh...

Beat.

Erm – did that payment go through?
Great.
And can I grab a bag as well? I don't have 5p.
Can I just have the bag – I can give it to you another time.
Please can – Just give me the fucking bag!
Thank you.

Just Go With It…
by Alex Theo

CHRIS, 19 years old; a Greek-Cypriot man-child. Born and raised in East London. Loves to banter and uses humour as an emotional blanket.

Daytime. Chris is sitting on a park bench. Wearing a track-suit, trainers, just casual all round.

Chris   I joined that Grindr like four months ago. It *proper* restored my faith in romance. You done Grindr? Basically, how it works is, you see a guy you like, send a message saying, 'Hi mate, how are you?' And they either block you, or send you a picture of their asshole… I was getting a bit fed up of seeing tunnels on the London underground, but then man like Javier came along. Fucking Javier, phwoar! He looked like a cross between Leo in *Titanic* and Leo in *The Great Gatsby*. Leo, I mean, Javier, was discreet like me – no one knows, except God, I guess. After chatting to him for two days straight, he mentioned he's having a party at his penthouse and asked if I'd like to come. He's a frickin' lawyer! I'm 19, thought it would be a good opportunity to meet, you know, more gays.

He lived in Catford, which was long, man, do you understand the trek? I live in Walthamstow, East London. Bruv I'd have been quicker travelling to

Cyprus (my home country) by boat, than South London. I kinda wish Ryanair did flights to South, tings would be much easier. I pulled up outside some house (I'm talking like I drive: man caught one train, three buses and another tram), got to the front door feeling like Frodo from *Lord of the Rings*. I get there and I'm like: this don't look like how he mentioned it; he was going on like he lived in Harrods. Why gas me saying it was a penthouse? Looked as if it was in the process of fixing, skip outside, tools everywhere, etcetera. No bell, door half-open, I walked in, stairs right in front of me. I could hear faint music. SIA's *Chandelier*. Mate, as I climbed the stairs I was shitting it. What if he didn't look like his pictures? You expect Obama, you get there and it's Trump. I couldn't deal with seeing a Trump, man. Den I *finally* fink: wait, what if he's a fucking murderer? Fuck it.

I opened the door, there he is. Obama, looking exactly like his picture. My willy tingled a bit I won't lie. It was kinda dark, just a couple of scented candles and some tea-lights placed here and there. I could see around 6 or 7 guys. Everyone looked roughly in their thirties, except this one guy who looked around 70, wearing this silk purple suit, reminding me of Hugh Hefner. I dunno how to put this in a polite way, but he was getting proper fucked in the corner whilst giving me *that* look. I was proper fascinated, like say when you see something and you're like, nah… but you still watch it. Look, I was expecting a chilled get together; you know, like a game of Monopoly.

Javier approached. Before I could say anything I felt his soft 'get on my dick' lips kiss me. He had this fucking amazing body, man, looked like he trained in the gym 23 hours a day, including legs. (I know, rare). I didn't mind him kissing me, but all his mates were there, was kinda awkward. But still I was like, 'fuck it'. We kissed and kept kissing for like ten min straight. I started feeling as if people were getting closer around me… I then felt these pecks on my neck, my arms, my back, was bare confused, cos Javier's left hand was on my chest, and his right was behind my neck. I jilted slightly, but Javier pulled me back, stared right into my eyes, holding my hands tight, and whispered in my ear, 'Just go with it.' I was praying it weren't that old man kissing my back up, allow it (I ain't ageist, I promise.) Javier started undoing my belt. I'm young; I'm living it up, innit? My right ass cheek went cold. I felt this hand really grabbing my right cheek – proper in the Calvins, no shame, just straight in. One thing going through my mind at this point was, if that gets any nearer to my, you know… so I kinda tried to turn around but Javier grabbed to kiss me more… Listen, I felt like I was this mermaid yeah? Who had been captured by this octopus in the ocean, whilst not being able to breathe under water, you get me? I started to feel something warm and blunt pushing between my, you know... Javier's tongue down my throat, my eyes wide open... Surely I wasn't about to get fucked?

I was the attention, the guy in the middle, like when you go to a party and that dead dancer gets in the middle and everyone's forced to cheer him. This tongue kept moving up and down my back slowly. Javier's eyes were still fixated on mine. 'Just go with it'. I felt like I could trust Javier, I barely knew him. But those eyes... *Just go with it*. I started searching for the moment to say that word – you know *that* word. The word. Say that fucking word. *Just go with it*. I go gym, I'm a strong guy, you know. I lift 30kg on each arm. You know? Yeah... but when there's 100kg pressing up on you, you just, you just...

I'd always imagined an orgy, you know, growing up relying on my right hand and my imagination; bunch of hotties all getting with each other. But this wasn't how I imagined nuffin. There I was, subconsciously praying to whoever the fuck was listening out there, that it was rubber instead of skin. *Just go with it*... So, that's how I lost my virginity. How about you?

Karen: H R Manager
by Verity Sharp

KAREN: 45, female, head of HR at P & G. Sure of herself, manipulation comes easy to her, extremely personable and charming.

Karen is sat at her desk in her office, checking herself in a handheld mirror. There is a knock at the door.

Karen Come on in.

Jodie, 24, enters and sits across from Karen.

> So, Jodie. Your three-month review. You've really settled in well, especially considering how young you are. Consistent. Punctual. Professional. It's been a real pleasure having you on the team and your presence in the office – in fact, while we're on the subject, can I just say on behalf of everyone, thank you for bringing herbal teas into the staff kitchen. Yay! I for one don't think I could ever go back to bog-standard English Breakfast now. So! I think it's safe to say that if you are enjoying yourself here, you have a job for life! Haha! Just one question: Would you like to get a drink with me?

Silence.

I checked your diversity form, and on there you stated that you were gay. (*Stands up and slowly moves behind Jodie, starts playing with Jodie's hair.*) It's nice to see you're so... at ease with your identity. You know... I just got divorced myself and I feel ready to try... *everything*. So, as shrewd as you are, I'm sure you've noticed I've been keeping an eye on you, you little minx. A very close eye. Don't worry, I won't tell anyone about that printer you stole – that's just be between us. Now. Let's go and get that drink.

Long silence.

(*Offended*) Should I be taking that as a 'No'? Sorry, I'm confused because I thought you liked women and your emergency contact is your mum so I'm guessing you're single?
So, what's the issue? Age? Am I too old? You're looking for an Ellen Paige and I'm Ellen Degeneres? Or what? I'm too femme? or too butch? Or too cis? Oh, yes, I know the jargon! I've cut my hair, committed to tailored worksuits. Am I still just too fucking straight? No need to explain. Obviously, you're not interested. And why would you be? You look like fucking Helen of Troy and I shop exclusively at Matalan. (*Exhausted*) I just thought you could at least consider me as a bit of fun.

Long pause.

If you report any of this I'll be forced to tell them about the printer. And the home shopping on the computer. Some interesting items on there for such a wholesome-looking little wench.

You've really stitched yourself up, haven't you, doll? You could have had something cushy and now you'll always be looking over your shoulder.

And all it would've took was one drink. I almost feel sorry for you.

Well, that's that for this month.

See you at your next review.

Princess.

KFC, Legs and Nine Cats
by Eloise Kay

Alex   Can you just stop and listen? Please? Thank you.

Look, I don't see the world like you do. Like most people seem to. I don't have those Disney 'love at first sight' moments, or even 'lust at first sight'. Never have. I don't do that automatic categorisation when I meet people – weighing up people's features and deciding who's attractive and who isn't. What would be the point? I could bump into the entire population of Britain and not feel anything for anyone. No blush in my cheeks, no butterfly rush in my tummy, no goosebumps. Just, 'Oh look. A person.'

There's no 'numbering' system, except to figure out how many people are in front of me in a queue. I couldn't give a toss how pert someone's arse is or how toned their abs are. I don't drool over legs unless they're covered in a blend of eleven secret herbs and spices and being sold by KFC.

Sex isn't important to me. It's not that I don't like doing it with you. Obviously, I like to do anything and everything with you – I love you. It's just... I don't really crave it as an activity, you know? Not detached from a person that I love. Like, I could never do a one night stand. Well, I mean, I could, technically, but I wouldn't. It'd be like eating an ice cream flavour I don't like because it's hot out and I think I should probably eat ice cream because that's what you're supposed to do. Pointless.

And I know it's not the same for you, I do. So it's hard for you to believe that you could be away for so long and I wouldn't have at least tried it with someone else, and I understand why you'd think that when I spent the night at his, something happened...

But for me there's just you. Only your smile makes me breathless. Only your voice makes me weak at the knees. You could disappear for decades and no one could replace you. It'd just be me and umpteen cups of tea and – I dunno... nine cats.

I've never looked at anyone else because there'd be no point. I'm not wired that way.

Kweenship
by Tom Wright

Emmanuel   One night, like way back, like six months ago,
when I was just a baby queen on the scene, I was on
a comedown, as per, in some shit-hole club off Old
Street and could not fucking deal with hetties chatting bollocks at me, so I flounced off towards home
on my own in these massive fucking gorgeous heels.
Disguising the wobbles like you do. Successfully
turning a trot into a strut. Forcing Beyoncé into
retirement. Yaaass!

And boom. Sat under the canal bridge, inside a
soggy cardboard box, there he was. Shaved peanut
head. Exquisite Bambi eyes. Even younger than I
was, and I was fucking young. I'm minding my
business, relishing a highly skilled, inconceivably
subtle, peripheral perve, when Bambi springs up
and hurtles straight at me. I didn't know if he was
making a clumsy pass – like all the straight boys do
– or if he was going to punch me – like all the
straight boys do. But he slips his arm through mine
and begins helping me walk in these fucking heels.
'Need a bodyguard to help you get where you're
going, hen?' I melted. Those eyes! 'Roamin' is
warmer than sitting.'

I called him Scotch Sam and he called me Cherub.

Even asked my pronouns. 'I flourish beyond the confines of binary language,' I elucidated. He un-hesitatingly ripostes, 'Aye, even Shakespeare's timeless virtuosity cannae surmise such peerless beauty,' in that thick Scots accent. Gag. We pass right through a throng of macho yobbos and this miraculous boy gently – no, *proudly* takes my quivering hand and smiles at them, and... they part for us. Practically bowing.

I daren't ask why this prince was homeless, but we were somehow unexpectedly extraordinary and I wanted to help him. Naturally I asked if he did drugs. He'd tried crack, but it made him paranoid so he don't fuck with it. Smart. Though he did like weed. Snaps! 'I've actually got some on me, princess. Maybe Ah'll be invited inside your hoose and we can shneeb a wee doobie together?'

We're at the stairwell of my hostel and I'm think-ing... Girl, wait. You don't actually know this man. Y'know what I mean? I'd been bashed before, and my most recent, still-healing scars were a valentine gift from a psycho ex-boyfriend. One minute him and I were deep tonguing on my chartreuse rug, the next he serves full Freddie Krueger, pins me down and gobs a greenie in my lashes. Adamant I'd lied about who I was – which I never do... Never trust a butch bitch. They can switch.

'I'm sorry handsome, but I've gotta be a bit careful here.' His face. Those eyes. Gutted. We smoked on the street outside my 'bit' – that's what he called it – him still smiling. Me watching. Guilty as fuck. Wishing I was more naïve and trusting. I wanted to get his number. Make plans. Maybe even kiss. But now my front door is closing on my buff Bambi bae. 'Bye for noo, canny cherub.' 'Night night, bitch.'

Lesbian Bar Story
by Dee McIntosh

Dee   Have I told you the lesbian bar story? Oh my god, it's great, listen. Okay, so confession: I did not meet a lesbian until I was fifteen – I know, it's ridiculous, don't laugh – so up until then I had no frame of reference for who I was or what was happening to me. I know it's a cliché but I'm from a small town and being gay isn't really a thing there, like we don't have support groups or meet ups or anything like that – to be honest I kinda thought we were going extinct or something.

Anyway, so, when I was, I think, seventeen, there was this show on about these women working in something called a lesbian bar and it blew my baby dyke mind. At the time I totally thought, well, that's impossible, there aren't enough lesbians to fill a bar and even if there were, as we all know if there are too many lesbians in a room together the universe implodes, I mean that's just science. Yes, I realise how dumb that sounds but you get the idea, I was sceptical. But I googled it and Christ, I learned some things I was not ready to learn, turns out search terms are VERY important. Anyway, I learned the shocking fact that it was not a myth and there were places where people like me could go and have a good time. So, basically I'm saying that the only reason I moved to London was to go to a lesbian bar, which sounds like a bit much but I was determined.

Okay, so it's a year later, I'm in London, standing

outside the very place that had been the source of all my hopes and dreams. I want to tell you that I was the epitome of nonchalant, but honestly I was shitting myself. So I take a deep breath, step in front of the entrance – and then promptly run away. So then I try again, I go up, peek in the door, and again, I turn and run. Pathetic, I know. Forty-five minutes later, I finally manage to take a deep breath, walk through the door, and the first thing I see... is a man. Sat at the bar, drinking a pint and reading a newspaper and he was, like, the only one in there. So that day I learnt that if you go to basically any bar before 9 p.m. they don't tend to be the liveliest of places. So, I obviously went back later, and everything looked pretty much the same with just a few more people, so I was ready to be disappointed. But then I went into the basement. And fuck me it was amazing – like, I know this is a super gay reference, but I felt like Dorothy when she gets to Oz and suddenly everything's Technicolor – it was just like that. And for the first time my life isn't in sepia, I can see colour. But all the time I'm in there all I can think is, 'Oh my god, I don't know how to be a lesbian. Oh god, what if they all find out I'm not gay enough and they ask me to leave.' Which was especially weird considering that for most of my childhood I was worried about being too gay. But in there in the crush of drunk, sweaty women dancing to music that only sounds good at one in the morning when you're hammered, I was finally unselfconsciously myself. In that moment, I was home.

Lesbian Fairy
by Maeve Scullion

Fairy   Hello, my love.

I've been waiting for you, in the grass,

In the clearing of this green, enchanted wood.

You're safe here.

I saw you when I climbed to the top of the trees,

and gazed into the sky.

Your world looks so different.

So painful.

So painful, for you.

I know what's in your heart.

I know you yearn for someone, something like me.

An entity full of light, and love.

We call it lightning.

You call it femininity.

I know in your world, people like you are punished.

Your purpose in life is to be loved by a man, is to

serve a man.

Is to perfect your skin, and paint your face, and

sculpt your flesh for a man – not for you and others

like you, but for men and the structures they create,

the stories they tell.

It doesn't matter how many seats they give you at

the table of power.

You are still

An object

A piece of meat

A servant
A doll
A dog.
You fear and are ashamed of the deepest and most
desperate desire of your heart:
The desire to be loved by one of your own kind.
In your world they punish you. You hide yourself on
the street, you fear attacks. You hide your life from
those who will not understand. You feel shame. You
feel afraid.
I saw him.
The shadow.
The shadow that followed you here.
The shadow that tried to engulf you.
The shadow that tried to cut you, to own you, to
devour you;
That threatened to pull you back before I could
open my mouth to you.
I approached him, waved my hand wide
And he was gone.
He has no power here.
Here, you can be free.
Here I will wrap my sweet arms around you.
Here I will trace my fingers through your long hair.
Here you can lay your head against the smooth
surface of my shimmering skirt
Feel my soft breath on your skin
My glittering wings will enfold you
You are safe here, in this place. I will adore you. I

will love you. I will keep you warm.

Come, look at the daisies and the bluebells.

Why not lie down here with me, on the soft, warm
ground?

Lynx Africa and Dildos
by Simon Castle

Jack   Darren, put the dildo down. I'm not going to hurt
you and I promise I'll try not to kiss you again.
It wasn't on purpose. It wasn't even a thought, I just
did it – and I know it's weird, but every Wednesday
in the changing rooms the scent of your Lynx Africa
goes straight up my nose and fuck, I've never loved
a boy before, but I was like, if that's what they smell
like – Lynx Africa and teenage sweat, then count me
in.

I didn't mean for it to come out like that. Look,
Darren, just wait. Ever since we were kids I knew
you'd be my best mate for the rest of our lives. I
want to play rugby with you forever, man. I want to
sit on the sofa with a Domino's and watch a game
together, and I want to go on shit holidays with you
in Cornwall because we can't afford to go abroad. I
want to go to university and be better than I am, in
the hope that I'll be good enough for you. I want to
watch you fail and fight, and argue with you. I want
you to hold me down and make it so I can't move. I
want to teach my kids how to catch a ball, I want to
teach our kids how to ride a bike. I want to drink
cold cider riverside while you swim. I want to feel
your body moving on mine. I want to wake up and
see you under the covers. I want your dad to walk
me down the aisle 'cause mine won't. I want to

taste every centimetre of you. And I want to have sex, vulnerable and rough, grunting and panting like animals. Because you make me feel complete.

In that heartbreakingly brief moment you were everything that has ever existed, and I don't know if it's that stupid, wonderful deodorant or the way you look holding that dildo – all manly and terrified – but I just want to be you. I just want to be you. I just want to be you being loved by me. 'Cause when it all gets too much, and I feel sick and dirty looking at my reflection, I think of you and just want to scream, 'You make it okay to be gay!' 'Cause you do. You make it okay to like boys and rugby. And dildos. So please either walk out that door or please kiss me. Because if all this makes me gay, I don't give a fuck. I just want to be with you.

My Mum, Her Man, and Auntie Rose
by Daniel Reid-Walters

Montell   I should thank you really, shouldn't I, Mum? Yeah, of course I should. Where are my manners? So, thank you. No honestly, thank you so much, Mum. I'm so grateful, so overwhelmed that you would do all of this for me. You've emptied my bedroom, packed my bags, brought them downstairs, put them by the front door. I mean, what a loving and sweet gesture, Mum. But I can't even stop there, can I? That's how amazing and loving you are, the list is just endless. I need to thank you for finding me somewhere else to live too, finding another family to take me into their home, because I'm no longer welcome in yours. It serves me right, really, for daring to be...

Oh, are you crying? You're crying? Why? Is it because you're gonna miss me? Aww please don't worry Mum, it's not your fault. No. It's your amazing taste in wotless men, that's the problem. He can't handle the fact that your son's gay, so you've chosen to kick me out, in the hope that he'll stay around that little bit longer.

I have to ask though, is it him who has the problem, or is it you? His homophobia he wears on his sleeve, but yours, yours is the worst kind. Hidden within your silence, saying nothing as he raises his hand to beat me, again, and again, for who I am and who I love. But what a loving mother you are, ay!

Is he here actually? 'Cause since I'm moving out, you must have moved him in, right? You here, Dad? HELLO? Can you hear me, Dad? Mum, can I call him Dad, or would that make you feel uncomfortable? You win, old man, you've got me out of my own home, and managed to turn my mother against me, so congratu-fucking-lations. I see the sense in all of this now, I really do. Some parents would be so pleased that their child trusted them enough to be open and honest with them, wouldn't they? About something no one should be ashamed of, or something that's actually irrelevant to them as a parent, BECAUSE IT DOESN'T AFFECT THEM. But not you, not my amazing mum.

You know Auntie Rose, your sister? She was the first person I told. I said, 'Auntie, I'm gay.' You know what she did? She grabbed me by my shoulders, pulled me in and held me, tight. Then she said she couldn't care less. She goes, 'You're still one of my babies, and you always will be.' I'm not even hers. What a difference there is between the two of you. We should call her, shouldn't we? Make her come over here, and you can tell her what you're doing to her baby. Who happens to be your son. Nah, why bother? She'll find out in time. And you can both have a lovely chat all about it, I'm sure she'll have lots to say.

I am sorry, Mum. For thinking you were ready. To know me. All of me. And for giving you the chance to choose me. I'm sorry for that. And the truth is, I should hate you for this. For all of this. For everything I'm feeling. Everything I'm losing. But I don't.

I love you Mum.

Bye.

My World
by Anthony Selwyn

Jordan I don't know what happened, officer! We were just messing around, you know, role play stuff, and then – suddenly I'm here. Fuck!

Okay.... *(Breathes)* Sorry.

Darren liked to... play. Sex games. I called him daddy and I was his boy, he'd keep me clean shaven, give me housework, cooking, cleaning – he liked me in a maid outfit. I looked good.

He'd create scenarios. Pimp and rent boy, Police officer and young offender – tracksuit, gold chain, body searches. You know how that works, yeah? Hehe. Anyway, being controlled like that by someone so much more experienced, finally belonging somewhere, to someone who couldn't get enough of me – of all the drugs he introduced me to, that was the biggest rush.

It got pretty wild. Like the night he made me climb into an air vent and he shut me inside for an hour with the aircon on full blast. After, when he let me out, shivering, half-blind, he had sex with me, made love to me. He called me his 'sweet baby' as he fucked my rigid body. I don't know how long I lay there on the cold kitchen floor.

Have you ever loved anyone that much? That you would become anything for them? I needed to know how much I could take – for him. It was my way of showing how much I loved him, you know? And I knew if I carried on he could never leave.

So you see? I could never...

I've always been a bit nervy. And, well, lately I've been getting these twitches, or maybe you'd call them outbursts. Like if a door shuts a bit too suddenly, I'll scream. Or this one time someone pushed past me in the Underground and my arms just went up in self-defence, and somehow I scratched his face. Tore right through his eyelid.

Anyway, last night... Darren brought a knife into the bed for a little rape fantasy. And I thought yes, this is it, the next level. My chance to prove my worth. So this knife's at my neck and he's pushing himself inside me and he's biting and making his animal noises in my ear, and then he's choking me, really choking me, and it goes on and on. Panic starts to flood my whole body, like I'm ten metres underwater and I'm flailing my way toward the surface to fill my lungs before they fucking implode. That's when it all goes black.

I wonder if I'm dead.

Then all of sudden I'm back – gasping, looking down at my lacerated hands. I look for Darren. He's not in the bed, He's on the floor, writhing in his own blood, which is just spraying absolutely everywhere from this deep, deep cut he's trying to hold together with, with his fingers.

I couldn't move, officer. I was paralysed. I just... sat and watched the confusion and shock in his eyes fade away until he was gone. He was still hard. I couldn't move or look away, I just sat there like a sentinel watching over him for... I don't know how long – until the room lit up blue and red, and I'm not sure if I was screaming this whole time or if it was just the sirens... and rough hands tore me away. Now you're telling me I've killed my boyfriend. But I could never hurt Darren. I loved him. I would have stayed here forever, with him. He was my world.

O-Fucking-Kay
by Shakira Newton

Farrah *(Shouting up at window)* Is that it?! I'm declaring my love to you, Romeo and Juliet style, and all I get back is 'okay'?

O-fucking-K. Is that all I am to you? Shakespeare's rolling in his grave... or tomb? *(To self)* Wait, did he get cremated?

Look. We haven't spoken in three days. That's the longest I've ever gone, in the six months of having you in my life, without seeing your name pop up on my phone.

Nayla, what did I do wrong? *(Listens)* ...Well no, 'cause I obviously have.

Is it – is it because I said we are 'just friends'? Because that was stupid. We have never been 'just friends', 'just friends' don't kiss each other with tongues and touch each other's lady gardens, which we have been doing for like three months now, so yeah, that was shit of me! No, I will not keep my voice down!

I LOVE YOU! I. LOVE. YOU. Even when you're making that angry, scrunched up face. I love that little scrunched up face. It's the same face you make in your sleep when your hayfever's playing up. You know I even love it when you sneeze? It's like this massive build-up of an inhale followed by a tiny little laser gun *(Imitates the 'pewm' of a laser gun)*. I love this flat. It stinks of piss and rotten food out here, but in there – in there is a museum of you. It's my happy place. *You're* my happy place.

What? No, I haven't been dri... Okay. Yeah. I have a little bit, but that doesn't invalidate my feelings!

I don't care that your neighbours can hear me! Why do you care?

(Looking around and realising.) Oh, is *that* it? Is that *actually* it?! Miss 'everyone should be what they desire to be'.

(Defeated and apologetic) Look, I get it. I'm not here to out you. I'm here to out myself. And you – but mostly myself! You don't have to do that. You don't even have to love me back. Just please. Please. Talk to me.

Outside the Head's Office
by Mical Nelken

Erika   Two minutes. I am strong, I am confident, I command respect. Why am I shaking like a naughty child outside the headteacher's door? Please, let someone else do this. Why do I have to do this, expose the unacceptable? How do I even start? Sorry to bother you, sir, but one of your senior teachers is a bigoted cunt? Who am I to complain about homophobia anyway? Will I look crazy? Maybe I am. I did just cry for thirty minutes. Oh God, what if he can see that? How do you come out to your boss? Is it unprofessional? Maybe I'm not even really bi. I mean, I have a boyfriend. Everyone knows I have a boyfriend.

Fuck, one minute. I am strong I am confident I command respect. 'Sir, I need to report a homophobic incident.' Good! Okay, it was mostly biphobic, but... let's keep it simple. How do I know? I can't give him names! I'm not outing my babies. But then what proof do I have? I'm just a crazy teacher who fantasises about being queer! That's what she said about me. Maybe she's right. Maybe bisexuality is, is in some way less than straight and not as good as gay. Confused. Confusing. Indecisive. Greedy, that's what she said. Maybe, maybe that's why it doesn't feel good. It doesn't feel good. Make it feel good. Breathe, breathe, breathe –

Oh, hi, sir! Nothing, sir. It's just… I need to report, sir… an incident. A serious incident.

I need to report a homophobic incident.

Poo Brown Eyes
by Alex Britt

Leanne I haven't *slumped* anywhere, I've always felt this way. Always. Yes, even when we were together: I've always had the capacity to be able to ravage a sausage roll just the same as I can a Cornish pasty.

Whatever – look, I'm a fucking adult, I'll have both at the same time if I want to. And I have, so... So don't stand there and tell me I've *defaulted* back to what society has conditioned me to like.

Because I've not died.

When I see a beautiful – a fucking Aphrodite-like specimen of a woman, just walking down the street, on her way to – I don't know, Aldi or wherever – I haven't lost the urge to imagine what it would be like to hold her in my arms and kiss her. Or stopped wondering what she would taste like in my mouth. How she would smell up close. Or wanting to see her eyes roll into the back of her head because I've made her cum like no man ever could. Like it was with you.

None of that has gone away, just because I'm with him now.

Like for fuck's sake, I still think about your vagina. A fucking lot.

Sometimes it just pops into my head when I'm

having a shower, or I'm, you know... doing Pilates or whatever, and I just think, *God what a bloody lovely vagina that was.* But then I have to remind myself that I shouldn't be thinking about that anymore. Not because it's forbidden fruit, or, because I've changed sexuality all of a sudden – but because we're not together anymore. And it's not good for me.

Anyway, whose fault is that?! You were the one who – okay, no, I don't want to get into that again.

So, just... just know that I love him now. Like I loved you. And... I'm not ashamed of it. I'm not ashamed that I love him, and I'm not ashamed *we* loved each other. That's the duality that people like me have. We can have that. And I'm proud of it.

So, please don't try to take away what we had. Or diminish it. I'm used to people diminishing who I am. I stayed quiet when people assumed my sexuality because we were together. And I'll probably stay quiet now when people assume it because I'm with him. But you... I can't have you do that. Because you knew me better than anyone. You still do. We're just not in love anymore. Let's face it, we're not. Are we?

You're still the best shag of my life – Chris doesn't make me cum like you did, I'll admit that, but... I do love him. Imperfections included. I guess.

Except...

Do you know what I really wish? I wish that I could take your eyes with me everywhere. I could forgive you almost anything because of your endless deep-sea blues. Cos Chris – well, he's got eyes like mine...

Poo brown.

I mean, they're just not quite the 'Ebony Eyes' that Stevie Wonder sings about, are they? There's just something... like, they don't quite...

Beat.

Look, I just really wish that from this moment on-wards, every time I saw him, he had yours. Because I got lost in yours a long time ago... and sometimes it still feels like I'm still struggling to get out.

But... I will. I have to. Because I love him, so I'll learn to live without them.

PROM KING AND A CAN OF K
by Saffia Kavaz

Beth   Miss Costello is a maths teacher, not a counsellor, and I don't need to see her. There's no –

Sorry.

There's no issue to discuss about my drinking in school, so can I go now? I requested a Celine Dion song.

Alright, I bought the can of K, okay? I don't know. I just...

I wanted to dance.

And shed this sheath from my skin.
And shout to the DJ, who ironically is also Miss Costello, 'Play Robyn.'

And dance on my own, in between the graceful girls with broccoli bodies and unshaven heads and not feel like a prick stick in a dress.

And I don't know, maybe buck up the courage to say, 'Look, I actually like you Chlo, and I don't just want to be friends –'

Erm, did I say her name?

Beat.

I just wanted to, you know, fuck things up a bit – sorry, Miss, language – but in a fun, messy way. Like tomorrow morning I'll say, 'Can't believe I snuck cider into prom. Bussin' moves from group to group, I am the pivotal point in this room, unapologetically crowning myself prom king, jumping simultaneously like we're in the pit at Wembley, did you see when I done the splits?' Not, 'Weren't it shit, I spent the whole time thinking, *I wish I could just be myself.*'

I don't know how to explain it to you.

I feel like... a room.

Today we were playing dodgeball in that P.E hall; now they've screwed in a few LED lights from B&Q and called it a disco.

Miss, this might be the ethanol, but, I *am* the PE hall.

For a night everyone gets to come out of their shell, and I have to crawl into mine and pretend. Play literal dress up, and fabricate some sort of emotion for house music. I needed a buzz of tenacity and certainty. And it came in the shape of an eight per cent tinny.

I'm sorry. Please don't ring my mum. She'd –

Well, you've met her.

Pritt stick? Pritt. Oh. Always summink new to learn.

Beat.

Do you know what, Miss, this was kind of a nice chat. Do you want to crack open another?

Kidding.

It's all coming back to me now. I gotta go.

Push Pops
by Naomi Denny

MAX (22) is standing leaning on the school gates, fidget spinner in hand. He looks up and straightens up as Alex approaches.

Max   Oh. Hi, Alex. You alright? Yeah, yeah. No, good. I haven't seen you in ages round here. You look different. You look – good.

Yeah. Yeah, just watching Lulah. Trying to give Dad some time off, he's not been right since – well, you know.

Nah I haven't heard from her. I'm fine with it. Good riddance in my opinion. But Lulah – yeah. It's tricky. She doesn't get it, she keeps asking where her mum is. (*Notices his sister is on the top of the monkey bars*) Oi! Lulah! Careful up there, yeah? Break your neck and you're not getting a Push Pop from the corner shop! (*Turns back*) But you know kids, sweets and playgrounds will distract them, at least for a little bit.

It's good to see you anyway, man. Yeah, no worries, we'll talk soon.

His sister runs up to him.

Fun? Yeahhhh! You're like a bloody monkey you are.

He struggles for a moment to focus.

Hang on a second Lulah, I just need to do something.

He runs after his friend.

Alex? Look man, I just wanted to say I know it's been a while and I know you've probably forgotten everything about me but I'd really like to see you again – Lulah, hang on a second I'm talking – if you're up for it. We had a great time before – Lulah, please! – sorry, and I know it's hard for you to be seen out with someone like me – not now, I'm talking! – and I totally get that, man, it's a big thing for me too so I thought – Lulah, come on, stop playing about, you're being annoying now – sorry, where was I, if you wanted maybe we could meet somewhere a bit more private, you know, and – LULAH FOR GOD'S SAKE JUST SHUT UP A MINUTE!

Someone else approaches.

Lucy.

Hey!

Haven't seen you in ages girl how are ya? Ah, that's great mate. What are you doing here?

A moment of realisation. He tries to cover it.

Mate why you going out with this bell-end? You sure you're feeling alright? (*Laughs*)

Nah we were just catching up. I'm watching this one right now.

Yeah, yeah – go ahead.

Alex? It was good to see you man.

A look passes between him and Alex. Max watches the couple leave, then approaches his sister, who has run off in a huff.

Lulah? Lulah. C'mon hon.

I'm sorry, okay? I'm really sorry. I shouldn't have shouted at you.

Shall we go home now? Get that Push Pop?

Yeah?

Nah, she's not there right now munchkin.

But I'll let you watch Scooby when we get in.

Rainbow Cupcakes
by Chris Woodley

Chanel I'm pissed! Miss, who's gonna run The Pride Group
now? You can't leave. Nah, I ain't having it. You led
the school Pride march last year. That day was mad!
People were c-raazy. I found rainbow glitter in
places I didn't know I had places. I mean, some girls
got to know those places if you know what I'm
saying, but I ain't spilling the T. Hah, that day was
mad! But the night, the night was lit. My flag's still
in my bedroom, you know? Just being there was…
Like, hardly any secondary schools went. Except us
lot, Miss. Hackney High represented! Brap-brap-
brap! (*Beat.*) I can't even deal right now. You wanna
leave? Miss, you pushed the school to have black
and brown in the rainbow flag. You made it feel
like… our twinkle and shine was real. I've never felt
that.

Tell me, who's taking over? Oh my days, it best not
be Miss Boyson! Nah, I don't trust her, no way man.
She never wears her rainbow lanyard, plus she's off
sick and shit. Sorry. I mean, she's never in and that.
School can't go backwards! Yesterday I had to tell
Teddy Bolter's football team to wear their rainbow
laces. Aaa-gain! Those wastes have already forgotten my LGBTQ assembly. Pricks! If they ain't wearing them at the match on Friday I'll tie Teddy's tiny
balls up in B block. But Miss you've done so much

with the Pride Group, more than any other teacher has. Just go part-time. Stay? (*Beat.*) I ain't gonna beg. Sure, I did when I wanted to run the Queer Cake Sale. But the whole school knows Nadine Forsyth would have fucked it right up. I said *mucked*, Miss. I mean come on now, I *killed* that cake sale. Those girls *loved* my cupcakes! My cupcakes got rinsed!

Here's some rainbow realness: I'm *not* having some straight replace you, I swear down. No way. No breeders allowed. (*Beat.*) Miss, I can say that! Well I think you'll find that I just did. I'm not having no straight teacher lead the Pride Group. Nah man. They need to be queer. I'm maybe okay with the ally thing, but a straight teacher ain't running the show. Nah. They're always running all the shows. Always there with their gluten-free brownies and sourdough breads. They wouldn't know a rainbow cupcake if I shoved it up were their rainbow ring-a-ting-ting. Please stay.

Tears? Nah, my eye's just watering. I got some perfume in it at break. I'm fine. (*Beat.*) Miss, you're the only lesbian I know that bare listens to me. You won't see me through my last year of A levels now. Or tell me what uni to go to. Coz my mum's never been the greatest at…. doing the mum thing. Pride Group's been like my family. So… I'll keep marching, yeah. (*Beat.*) I gotta go detention, Miss Boyson caught me shouting 'Teddy Bolter's got a tiny bell-end' at break. She was pissed. But Miss, just wanna say thanks for… seeing me. Oh, and remember, those girls *always* gonna love my rainbow cupcakes.

Respect
by Dian Cathal

Reiley Look Jess, you're either being stupid or rude. And honestly, I gave you the benefit of the doubt and went with stupid because you're my friend and you can't control being stupid. The human brain is a miraculous machine that records more than we can ever know, but if your brain literally lacks the ability to take in and retain information, I'd be a dickhead to hold it against you. But I know you're smarter than that.

You know exactly what you're doing. You're doing it on purpose. You know how to ask the pronouns of every dog you meet but you can't use mine? 'Oh, pronouns are hard.' Fair enough, a lot of people have that problem but usually they're toddlers.

And you can say 'I don't care about labels', 'live and let live', but you don't believe that. You're judgemental as fuck, Jess. It's why we're friends. You just don't want to look like an asshole right now. Which I get. It's why I don't correct you, because then I'm just 'attention seeking' and 'making it bigger than it is'. But I'm not. It's who I am, and that deserves attention. And to have to hear you say every fucking time I see you that who I am isn't worth the barest sliver of your attention and care is a big thing. Bigger than you will ever know. It's just mean.

If we worked together for five months and you couldn't be bothered to learn my name, there would be a secret office WhatsApp group to talk about what your fucking problem is. You've been my friend for ten years.

Imagine if I told everyone about the time you tried to use your bed post as a dildo? Why would I tell everyone that? It's who you used to be! And doesn't the whole world have the right to know? What if someone wants to sleep with you? It's my moral duty to tell them you might still have splinters inside you!

Pronouns aren't 'preferred', they are who I am.

I know I should expect it, the world sucks, it really does. But I really thought you would care enough to get over it. That I was worth the work of learning a new name. It's really not that hard.

So either you use your brain to record who I am properly, or just delete me completely. Because if you are incapable of learning that, you have no hope for learning the rest of me. Because who I am is fucking immense and more than worth your attention. And your respect.

Run Away, Bride
by Sèverine Howell-Meri

Izara   Jesus specifically told me not to do this. He told me
to stay till the fucking end and I couldn't even get
through the beginning, so Jesus took pity on me and
changed his mind.

Her friend Toyin turns to get help.

Toyin, stop. Please. I don't need your brother, I
need you.

No, not as my maid of honour. You're a brilliant one
but I mean I really, really need *you*. Going through
this with Ali isn't right. I'd rather be anywhere but
here, actually. I'd rather be somewhere with you.

Toyin, I tried so hard.

You know I went to church every single weekend. I
read and studied the Bible. Religiously. Why didn't I
walk out when I listened to the priest spew sermons
in confession about how I would go to hell? Why did
I let it get under my skin? Well, I swallowed his
spew and forced myself to keep it down because
letting it come up would have been so much worse.
But despite how much I tried, and I really have up
until now, the feeling just won't go anywhere –
especially when I look at you.

Like right now.

I know it's scary as hell. Literally as scary as Hell. But looking at you, all I want to do is be close to you, and promise I'll be with you for richer and for poorer and see you smile back as you say, 'In sickness and in health,' then hold your hand and walk down that aisle with you. With YOU, Toyin...

Oh fuck, T, please don't cry. Please don't cry, baby girl. I thought you knew. Hoped and prayed. Prayed and prayed and prayed so hard.

Who cares what our families say? Okay, I do care what they say – but they aren't the ones who will be coming home with me every single night, and they won't be the ones making any vows to someone who they aren't in love with. I'll always love you, Toyin. Just like I always have.

So, I'm leaving. And obviously I won't be alone if you come with, so will you? No one we know will ever understand but, honestly, I do not need them to understand. Because Jesus will. Jesus does. He told me. He said, 'Tell her. Then run.'
So I've told you.
And now I'm gonna take the side door. Take it with me? Me and you and Jesus?

See Yourself
by biogal_

take off your earring
slide it across the floor as an offering
take off your trousers
attempt to wear as top
breathe
show your face
say 'I had to tell her twice actually I had to tell her more
than that I had to tell her a lot I had to tell her all the
fucking time but we don't have much time so for the
purpose of this I had to tell her twice' twice
'that I'm trans'
spit into your hand twice
apply the spit to the corners of your eyes
'I am trans by the way unless that wasn't clear
what would it look like?'
what would it have to look like for her to hear me the first
time?
hear me'
cover your face with your trousers
say 'I'm not your son' until she hears you
see yourself
'that wouldn't have been appropriate this isn't appropriate
none of this has been appropriate'
'I'm gonna put my trousers on now'
put your trousers on your legs
'and then I'll leave this room and I'll tell more people I'm

trans over and over again in more and more ways all of
them appropriate enough'
'enough to let them forget'

s/he
by Liv Ello

she

she swirls the ice in her overpriced cocktail with a
now mushy paper straw
she
she laughs at sentences that weren't meant to be
funny
she laughs at the sentences I intended to be funny
she tells me about her job, her family
while I burn my beer mat in the candle
bit nervous
she tells me about her best mate Lily
who 'sounds like a laugh'
I say
sounding like a twat
she laughs
she touches my hand
she touches her hair
which I definitely read somewhere
means that
she likes me
I touch my hair too
the secret sex code continues
exchanging looks
we talk about books
bell hooks

poetry
politics
family dynamics
mothers
– hers is dying
she tells me, calmly
and I don't quite know what to say
we sip and stare at each other
she squints with a sharpness
maybe the amaretto sour
or uncertainty
scanning my shirt for chest or breast
to my hands
my throat
my groin
I flash a grin so violently it splits my lip
shit
sorry
she says don't worry
still finding me funny
with blood on my face
'I should go to the loo
and get some tissue
but then maybe we could go back to my place?'
she smiles and nods
as I walk to the toilets
the blood on my lip turns to strawberry jam smiles
the intoxicating sweetness of my body
delicious duality

I am the diner and the chef

fuck

M
or
F

No disabled access cubicle
separate from the binary
providing my usual dilemma relief
until my dramatic limps and hobbles are no longer
believable
but just plain offensive

glance back to our table
she is entranced by the glow
of her phone
I'm on my own

M for… maybe?
I enter with my eyes on the floor
pass the piss puddles and into the stall
to find a cardboard cylinder
I browse
no paper towels
just defunct dryers
and a guy at the urinal
we catch eyes

he smirks
I smile
and more blood trickles down my chin

I was probably about fifteen
when I found out my body to some was obscene
in between
a threat and disgrace
I made men feel disgusted and women unsafe
and things are hard enough when you're fifteen
trying to figure out what it all means
standing in front of a mirror
hips and tits and pubic hair
stuffing socks into my underwear
to feel a bulge
to feel something
to feel like me
footsteps on the stairs 'dinner's ready!'
bundled socks fly across the room
'I'll be down soon'
castrated for mum's carbonara

'tranny'
the guy mutters
and I dash for the door
because I already know
that conversation ends in more
blood
on my face

F for femming up my voice
'excuse me'
'sorry'
'is that one free?'
two women, mouths open in disbelief
'you're in the wrong place, this is the ladies
these toilets are only for women and babies'
I tear the toilet roll
one woman runs out
as the other grabs my arm
I pull away and spray
'fuck you' in blood all over her
'what's wrong with you?!'
what's wrong with me?
what's wrong with you
he
she
she-he'
security enters
'excuse me, you have to leave'
he grabs me
hurts me
feels me
shames me
and my body
my arms felt weak under his grip
matching bruises to go with the lip
he let me go

and I wanted to go home

she
she?
she was gone
replaced by a receipt by our seats
with a number on the back
and the words

'had to go, mum emergency.
fuck the binary, call me'

Shit on the Floor
by Lev Govorovski

Leo   I did a shit on the floor today. Not because I was desperate – I was literally metres away from a toilet where I could shit in peace – I did it 'cause I wanted to. I wanted to spite that stupid little greasy haired caretaker who stunk of forty years' worth of nicotine. I wanted him to come in here and use his bare hands to scrape my dried up faeces off the floor. I wanted Mister Caster to discover my shit, then vomit in horror as he saw the disrespect I'd shown towards his precious little school. I wanted those students who'd called me a poncey little faggot to walk into the boys' toilet, slip on my shit and end up covered with my now hour-old excrement. I wanted them to suffer, I wanted them to experience all the shit that I had been through, that I had lived through, I wanted them to feel my shit, and afterwards I wanted them to feel as shitty as I did. Honestly I wanted them dead, but they didn't deserve to die. It would be too easy. they deserved to be dragged through the shit. Through my shit. Through their shit. Through all the fucking shit in the world. I wish I could have done more, I wish they could feel it, but it's all over now and I'll never see them again. Maybe when I'm mega successful I'll come back and give a talk about how I made it, how I was a success story, how no one liked me, literally no one but I still came out on top, and I'd tell them to never give up, and to never let people put you down, and then I'd tell this story about shitting on the floor and I'd start a revolution of people shitting on the floor until the entire world would be shitting on the floor. Then finally I'd be normal...

But I don't want to be normal.

And I'm never gonna be normal, thank fuck. Because I've just done a shit on the floor.

Specifically Off-White Dunlop Sports Socks
by Louis Rembges

For a male identifying performer, to be read at speed. The formatting and capitalisation of the text is to help with delivery and pacing, but can be ignored.

Teddy   My First sexual experience with another boy was being masturbated by my cousin's foot every teatime under the table where my aunt and uncle ate, and the first time I came we were eating spag bol and garlic bread

and I thought of you, Dad
Which sounds disturbing but honestly it was fine
No one found out straight away
And I had an identical pair of three quarter length denim culottes in the bedroom I was staying in upstairs, so
It wasn't a bad summer
I just shouldn't have been there should I
Maybe the send off on my sexual voyage would have been emphatically more normal if I hadn't gone and shared a room with a budding six-pack on legs during that particular eight weeks northside of the solstice when heterosexual male teenagers are apparently on heat
No actually, no
I'm victim blaming again (this means I'm putting the blame Back Into Myself by means of a paternal inferiority complex)
Which I have been sternly told by Two therapists that I have to Stop Doing, so let me rephrase

I shouldn't have had to spend my year seven holidays just as my balls were dropping as a faintly sentient cum sock for a sixteen year old Family Member (your side) with the libido of a spoilt jack-hammer

Weirdly though, after my eleven year old summer as a impassive plimsole of love I only have one major kink

Which I find Remarkable

God it's much easier talking about this stuff in a graveyard, fab listeners

I haven't been interrupted once

Well Dad

The reason I'm here is

I'm here to tell you, now that you're gone

Thank you

Kicking me out slap bang in the middle of my forma-tive years into the instep of my horny, abusive and overdeveloped cousin

Thank You

For what you gave me

For something that I have because of you

Something I'll always treasure, and that will be bound to your memory as long as I continue to draw breath

Thank You Dad

For my foot fetish

Thanks to you, Dad, I cannot Cum without feet, without Feet I cannot cum

And if they're swaddled in specifically off-white Dunlop sport socks

I'll cum twice.

Stereotype Me
by Micah Holmes

Angel Do you know what I absolutely love? Being stereotyped. I adore it. In fact, that's my new favourite
hobby. I'm going to write it on my Tinder profile!
Hobbies and interests – being stereotyped.

My favourite thing to do on a Monday morning is to
wake up ridiculously early, have a venti caramel
latte from Starbucks, and subject myself to degrad-
ing criticism from someone that has never met me,
but can yet make an extremely informed decision
about my character based on a fifteen-minute
interaction where they paid more attention to their
croissant than me.

I was in such a good space. I walked out of that
building and strode towards the station with the
conviction in my belly that I had absolutely smashed
that audition. I had adhered to all the rules, I had
toned down my outfit, a white shirt tucked into a
black jean, my hair done neatly and conservatively,
no loud accessories. Nothing that could give the
impression that I was 'too much'. And yet, when the
phone went off, my heart was racing.

Palms clammy in nervous but positive anticipation, I
answer.

'Hi babe, it didn't go your way I'm afraid. Mr Parsons will not be casting you in this role. He said you were a bit too... effeminate.' Effeminate? No shit, Sherlock. Because I didn't pick up the script and think a window dresser smoking a fag ranting about his job would be a salt of the earth, football watching, beer drinking father of five boys. Silly me.

You see, unfortunately for the human race, the world doesn't view masculinity the way I view masculinity. I grew up with a mother who fought to put bread on the table for her slightly weird son and two daughters. Who pushed her son to go to ballet lessons despite the backlash from her friends, peers, and people who said it was 'for girls'.
My mother has bigger balls than any man I've ever met, and I respect the hell out of that. So forgive me if I don't grab my crotch, and manspread, and grunt with aggression. Who I am, who I love being has taken a journey that would have made these lads' Oysters spontaneously combust. Everyone's saying 'self love', 'positive state of mind', 'put yourself first'. Well I tell you what, babe, I'm practically a yogi, my chakras are that aligned.
The way I wear my varnish, the way hold myself, the way I present myself... Is all just one big 'fuck you' to a world that continually reminds me I am different.

'Wagwan bro, you good my g? The Arsenal game was mad, still! She's a MILF mate, she's peng! You got a lighter mate...?'

Don't chat to me about masculinity. I know her inside and out. I can imitate her all day long if you want. And she's a fraud.

Support
by Griffith Rees

Volunteer   Welcome to Student Support Service: we're here to listen.

How's your week been?

Could you please make a sound so I know you can hear me?
It doesn't have to be your voice. Some people find it easiest to just tap the phone.

Right. Thank you.
Are you in a place where you feel safe to communicate?
Okay. Thanks for confirming.

This may be a difficult question to answer, but all this is anonymous and confidential, except if a life is at risk.
Are you having any suicidal thoughts?
It's completely fine to take time to answer.

Thank you. Could you, could you just confirm that one more time?

Thanks.
Are you self-harming or considering self-harm?

Sorry I'm hearing something different but a bit like taps.

I know this can be difficult, but if you could pause, and then just clearly tap once or twice.

I can change the topic if that's too...
Could you please...
Excuse me.
I'm hearing heavy breathing now, and the tapping...

I've heard that sound before: that's not tapping is it. That's... Please stop that.
Your number will be banned and reported to security.

If this is – if this is Mike... How would you even know it's my shift tonight? Did another volunteer...? Are you the one who's been calling and quickly hanging up? Hunting for me?
I never thought that even you could get this brutal. 'Having fun,' eh? On my shift? Grunts, snarls, smirks in my work time. My space. And yet here we are again, servicing your pleasures, never mine.
And the yells. The shout of guilt disguised as blame you hurled the day I finally realised I was due someone actually kind. Who didn't fill me with rage. Who didn't make me afraid to open up and say what I needed. What I could offer. To touch and be touched in ways I never knew before. Held. Embraced. Real, un-faked, unforced, unashamed orgasms. Real, flustering attraction when I'm near

her. Real giggles, teases, tongues, tenderness with someone who loved me for my softness and never shamed or feared me.

Silence from you? No grunting. Panting?
Could this be what I waited for all that time we were together?
Are you actually – for the first time – listening? Interesting.
It doesn't sound like you're getting pleasure any-more.
I loved you, you know. For your mind, beautiful and sick as it could be and yes, your body. For those moments of debate when it felt like an intellect that matched mine. For those sweaty moments of potential vulnerability that you never allowed us to fully inhabit or explore.
But flirting with possibility is not romance. And we need that. We deserve both. Our sex was a punish-ment for daring to expose your tenderness. And all those teasing moments of possibility melted away from the day-to-day; and all the pain, all the shame, all the shuddering fear swallowed all the offers I made you. Strange it took this long to see it and speak it. Strange to feel clear enough and ready enough to say it now...
Are you ready to hear?
Are you there?
Are you listening?
I am. I'm listening.

Mike? I can't be with you, but I'm tired of hating you.

Are you in a place where you feel safe to communicate?

Could you please make a sound so I know you can hear me?

Thank you. Let's begin.

Take Five-Hundred-and-Ten
by Tom Ratcliffe

Note on text: Lines signify a new take of the video Jake is recording.

JAKE, 29, is in the process of filming a video profile for an online dating company specifically for those who have experienced grief at the loss of a partner.

Jake   Jesus am I really doing this?
Hang on.

Jake takes a moment to figure out his left from his right in relation to the camera. He calculatedly shifts a couple of steps to the left. Shifts his body on a slight diagonal towards the camera.

Okay yeah that's my good side.

Hi I'm Jake... I'm twenty-three... I'm a Pisces. I would describe myself as –

I look like a five-year-old of course I can get away with it.

Hi. I'm Jake. I'm twenty-nine. I. I think the most

accurate description of me is that I'm a guy's guy. A lad's lad. A man's manly man. A normal bloke looking for another normal bloke to live our lives together in a normal way. And to do normal things with. Like. Um. Rock climbing and paintballing.

I'm into sports you see. The gym. Big into football. Up the Liverpool United.

What the fuck am I supposed to say?

You can say 'be honest' all you like but honesty doesn't necessarily get you anywhere.

Like what? I'm supposed to say, 'Oh hey world. I'm Jake. I work at the National Trust. I'm about to hit thirty and I've just moved back in with my overbearing menopausal mother whose sole purpose in life, I believe, is to crush the remaining fragments of what used to be my self-esteem. Because even that – even that is better than the perpetual loneliness and endless sockwanks I've experienced ever since my ex got hit by a bus. I genuinely think I've forgotten how to have sex, and the last time someone touched me I came within twenty seconds before proceeding to cry into their pillow for over two hours straight.'

Sure, 'Help and guidance'. Sure. Now I bet everyone wants to fuck me.

Jake takes a deep breath.

He steadies himself.

Hi. I'm Jake. And this is this is take five hundred and ten.

I'm a twenty-nine-year-old Pisces and I'm quite insecure about that. Because I'm not necessarily sure about what I'm doing with or what I want from my life anymore. I lost my partner about... three years ago now. And as much as I've maybe felt ready, in some way, to meet someone new, or at least give that a try, I've found dating having gone through something like that at an early age pretty... hard. To say the least. So, the idea of meeting someone else who has... lost. Even in some way. Yeah. It seems like this is probably the best place for me.

I'm a home bird. I like making sourdough bread from scratch and having roast dinners at six o'clock sharp on Sunday evenings. I never cheat on Yorkshires and I spend more time on Animal Crossing than I do any kind of physical activity. I'm here

because as much as my –
As much as Sam impacted my life in such an astro-
nomical way, I haven't given up hope of meeting
someone else just as amazing, if not more amazing,
yet.

So if, for whatever reason, you haven't skipped on
to the next lost soul desperately looking to fill that
cold vacant spot beside them every night, and
aren't put off by a largely pessimistic outlook on the
human experience, then drop me a message.

That would be. That would be really nice.

Taste the Wine
by Nicole Cyrus

RILEY: male or female twenty-something, British-South American Bisexual/Pansexual.

Riley How on earth are both Steven and Evelyn here?

Is apprehensive the word?

No, I'm used to apprehensive.

Right now I'm downright agitated. The crowd can see it.

Ah, I can feel it! It's these stupid expressive eyes of mine.

Meanwhile Steven's eyes are peering through the corked bottle-tops clinking against his sleek jawline. He strolls up on stage with his boisterous ease, manoeuvering through the crowd with nine bottles of wine that look like tiny corkscrews in his gigantic hands and hugged to him by those forearms.

Damn.

Evelyn's there, tenderly setting up her wine glasses. She does this thing where she's staring at her bottles, and you can see the cogs of her mind racing behind her eyes, but her face is always stern, no expression. Did I just dart my gaze away, avoiding eye-contact too hurriedly? Judges aren't meant to be perceived as distressed.

Then somehow they both catch my eye at the same time, same amount of joy and affection. The same affection they've both put into fermenting their own wine for the last twelve months. The same affection and focus I should be putting into judging this home-brewed wine contest. The same labours of love they've each been giving me – and that I've been willfully splitting between them both.

Bollocks.

The two people I already feel sketchy about – okay, let's be real here; ashamed about – right in front of me – and three hundred other people. Including my lovely grandparents – after I've spent the evening licking Steven's belly hair and the previous morning caressing Evelyn's slender neck and shoulders... The first year I get to graduate from contestant to judge in the home brewing market and here I am on the brink of a sex scandal. Winemaking will never be so mundane again. We'll put all three faces on the bottle, our own signature brand of menage à trois. Easy on the loins and sultry on the taste buds.

Three hundred pensioners, all eager to learn the gracious secrets of the home brewing trade, and I'm sitting here assessing my bisexual escapades and whether Steven or Evelyn has fulfilled my kinkiest fantasy.

As if they can tell what's spinning through my mind, four feet high up here on this stage.

They're here to witness the majesty of my tastebuds as I dissect the subtle tones of each one of these wines up for the prize. Not whether I've tasted more of Evelyn's or Steven's sweat glands. Not whether I prefer the boldness of Steven's chest or the curvatures of Evelyn's hips. Not whether the tormenting confusion and shame has invaded the look of appreciation on my face.

I used to think romance was about who set your heart alight, who made you feel at home, who made you feel like all the fear and excitement and awe of life could be folded into one human being. Who can make me feel like they're everything I've ever needed, and everything I've been petrified of having my whole life. But now I just feel greed.

Who taught me that this was greedy. that being me could be gluttonous? But I guess it doesn't really matter now, I'm in too deep. Too 'greedy' to ever want to stop.

Thanks But No Thanks
by Reuben Massiah

Eddie Wow... so now you want to be here? Now you want to walk me down the aisle, smile with our *invited* guests and play happy families? Dad, your timing has always been off but this is... I gave you ample time to be okay with this. *You* chose to not meet Alex. You chose to tell me time and time again that you'd *never* be at my wedding. And today y*ou* are choosing to stroll in and cause trouble before the *most* important moment of my life. You don't get to demand a damn thing! You don't get to badmouth Uncle David for walking with me after h*e* stepped up when you *refused* to. DO YOU –

Takes a breath.

Do you know how long I waited to hear you say those words? That you wanted to support me, love me and be here for me. I wanted to hear all of that – nine months ago. And every time I called you up, asking for the bare minimum, you shut me down. And now suddenly you turn up, giving every reason under the sun why *you* deserve to be involved, but still have the audacity to start with, 'You know, Eddie, I can't say I'm happy with this but...' But what? Everyone here is happy for me, so why are you here if you're not? You don't get to celebrate the half of me you can tolerate and spit on the other part you hate. So thanks but no thanks, I'd actually prefer it if you just...

No. I refuse to let any more of *our* special day to be ruined by you. Alex is stressed enough as it is. So... Stay if you want. Make small talk. Make a grand speech at the reception. Tell my partner how happy you are to see us tie the knot. Or go out of that door, into the car park, and leave. It's that simple, Dad. Either stay and be happy. Or stop making a scene. And go.

The Goblin Prince
by Rory Howes

Dungeon Master With a flourish you swing your Plus
Twelve Sword of Severania into the neck of the
Goblin King, your biceps bulging heroically as his
head soars over the parapets. Cheers and screams
of joy fill the air. You pull off your helmet, letting
your long golden hair cascade over your broad and
manly shoulders, turn your handsome face towards
the village you've just saved, and bellow in your
deep, husky voice, 'The kingdom is safe! You, fair
people, are free once more!'

The crowd applauds, the people are saved, et
cetera et cetera. You take the hand of the Goblin
King's daughter, and... prepare to... um... ask her a
very important question. You drop to one knee and
– Actually wait. Sorry, there's a bit I've missed, um...
Here. Right.

Behind the Goblin King's daughter is the Goblin
King's son. He's not as pretty as her. He's kind of
small, and a bit weird-looking. He's wearing glasses
that are too big for him, so he has to stick them
behind his pointy ears with Blu-Tack. You ask him
what the matter is. The goblin clears his throat and,
with some difficulty, looks into your lovely, ocean-
blue eyes.
'I am very grateful to you for being here today,

brave warrior. I know this isn't normally your sort of thing, but it means a lot to me – to the village – that you came. And I wondered if... maybe you'd want to get a flagon of mead sometime?'

The goblin's being silly, of course. Just really stupid. I mean, a brave warrior like you has far better things to do on a Tuesday than drink mead with a scrawny goblin. But you smile at him. That really nice smile you do where the left side goes up a bit higher than the right. And you look at him. And you keep looking at him. And then...

Um.

Well, I actually don't know what happens then. That's up to you. Let's say... if you roll a ten or higher, you sweep the goblin off his feet and carry him back to your apartment, where you feast on microwave popcorn and watch *RuPaul's Hag Race*. Roll a five or higher, you tell the goblin you're very flattered but you've already been promised to his sister, which is totally fine, he gets it, it's like whatever, you know?

Roll below a five, and you punch the goblin in the chest, shattering his heart and leaving him to die a painful, lonely death. Okay?

The Dungeon-Master rolls.

Two. Right.

Ooh, except... Nope. You used your last resurrection

spell on that siren in the Erotic Cove so. There we go. Goblin Prince dead.

Well, then! That concludes this campaign. You've saved the kingdom, rescued the Goblin Princess and I see a bright future of prosperity and lots of really cute mixed-species babies. The Goblin Prince, meanwhile, washes away with the rest of the sewer water and his rotten remains are devoured by hungry river trolls. And that's it. Congratulations. I've been your Dungeon-Master. Thank you for playing.

Oh, you actually can't roll again. That would change the outcome of the quest, which is completely against the... rules...

Sure. Let's roll again.

Nine.
We can round that up to ten, right?

The Dungeon-Master smiles. The Dungeon-Master rolls again.

The Maiden
by Alexander Da Fonseca

Chris   Look at it. This. House is a mess. So messy it's
almost ordered.

Swimming pool's all choked up. Weeds.

Seems fitting. Spends his whole life devoted to a
Grade II glorified hut, goes shooting once, only to
have all his furniture pissed on by feral cats and
geese and chickens and.

Feels right to see it off. 'The prodigal son', all that.

Dad wouldn't have minded you here.
He was always keen I brought home a girl. So I
guess he'd be half-pleased. Or double. Is that a
thing? How do you identify?
You don't have to tell me. I don't care.

I just really like you.
I think he would've.
I don't talk about him to anyone so... you're get-
ting, yeah, special privilege.

If I'm wrong, go back.

Go on.

See. Kindred spirits.

Stay here with me. I can show you the woods, if you like.

Forest's the only logical place I can think of.

My hidey-hole.

I'd spend ages out there as a kid. Probably really healthy but it's just like a blank space. I think I used to just walk around. Doesn't it make you feel like that; feel your heart. The forest breathes so slow.

I envy you. You were off everywhere, inside it all. Living. I had to wait till I was somethingteen. To escape the provinces. Just to see England. Never another country, another man's body. Or a woman's. Or a girl's.

I was out here. With thecatsandthegeeseandthe chickens.

You're not scared are you? Zara, I'm not a virgin.

I'm not.

Not really.

It's harder being alone when you're supposed to be a man.

Isn't it.

Men tend to know who they are – OK that's a lie – men have to have an idea of what they want other people to think they're like, and then they're that person the whole time, that's who they are, who they think they are, like usually it's the funny one.

And it doesn't matter if they're not the funny one,
because they're always the funny one. I used to do
that.
Still do.

But I don't know anything about the queer thing.
I want to.

They used to think unicorns would only lie down for
a maiden. In the old country. Showed you were
pure of heart. They'd appear and bless you like
silver mist.

Looks up.

Rain.
Told you things change quick out here. It'll get dead
muddy. Might get trapped the weekend. If we're
lucky. Stay.

I do really like you, you know. I'm not lying. Not
about that. Truth is I am a bit of maiden. A man
maiden. Yet to be deflowered. Not that I've got a
hymen or anything but

Will you lie down with me?

The Pain of Being Honest
by Alistair Wilkinson

Oscar   I often think about that time when we were watching TV together, whilst simultaneously going through your Tinder, looking at potential matches for you. My head rested on your thigh and you had your arm around me. I felt so connected to you. I could feel our heartbeats sync and our breath felt like it was in a combined rhythm. For a moment, it was perfect.

But then I think about the actual strongest memory I have of that moment, which is watching as you swiped right for guys that looked nothing like me.

You said you saw me appear on your Tinder. I saw you too. I swiped right, but we didn't match. I was hoping we would've because it could've started this cute little awkward conversation about how funny it is that we are a match, and that could have led to a further, more serious and longer awkward conversation about us and where we're at. It could have been the catalyst for the huge elephant in the room that is our feelings towards one another. Both of us are too scared to make the first step, so this might have been our opportunity to do that. But you didn't swipe right, so... And you're probably not too scared to make any first step, because for you there isn't one to take. You're happy with how things are.

And that's fine, obviously, that's totally fine.

This morning your mum sat me down and said to me that you're never going to give me what I want to hear, and I need to decide what is more important – chasing the dream or living in the reality. The reality is that we're best friends, with the most *amazing* dynamic. My dream is that we are more.

I sit there and watch you talk to some guy online who seems to be able to give you things I am unable to. I listen as you tell me the story of how you were sexting with someone during an online rehearsal for the play you're in. I look as you scroll down one particular boy's Instagram, stalking his posts from years ago, smiling at things I'll never know about because his account is on private. Seeing and hearing these things makes me want to scream.
He isn't worthy of you. You deserve so much better.
You shouldn't be with him
You should
be with
m-

I know that I have the power to put a smile on your face too, but it isn't the same type of grin, which makes me feel kind of worthless, you know?

It's not your fault. The thing is, I know there is only a 1% chance of you feeling similar, and in the grand scheme of things that isn't a lot. However I've always fancied myself as a bit of an underdog when it comes to love. A bit of a chancer. But also, I suppose I've always been the best man and never the groom so...

But hey, maybe not this time? Okay, here I am, throwing the dice, hoping it lands the way I want it to.

Umm...
I like you
And I know you already know that, but for the first time I'm actively telling you.
I like you. A lot.

He'll never love you like I would. Like I do.
So, how about it? Would you, like to –

Because you've already got a match. Right here, with me.

This is It
by Benjamin Salmon

Samuel On three separate occasions, I tried platonically befriending three different gay men called David, Daniel and Dominic. And, let me tell you, each and every one of them was a bonafide cunt.

And, because I clearly had no self respect at the time, I tried everything you can possibly imagine to get those vile twats to like me.

First, I tried being gayer, which involved me trying to be camper, which didn't go down well because gay men are evil, so then I tried not being camp whatsoever.

Then I tried pretending to love myself. Then I tried being a slut. Then I tried bondage. Then I tried bragging about all the weird sex I was having. Then I tried developing a mild cocaine addiction – which turned out to be the most successful technique. Then I tried drinking water instead of eating lunch. Then I tried spin classes. And then I went and shaved off all my pubes, which ended up with me having a long overdue cry, temporarily giving up on life, eating whatever the fuck I wanted and masturbating three to seven times a day.

I've spent my twenties trying to fit in with people like cunty Dominic, Daniel and David, or some other bitch who thought he was the gay Naomi Campbell. I tried so much and not a single one of them wanted to be my friend – and I'm a hoot. I am a literal hoot.

And I'm not having a go at any of them, I'm not having a go at gay men, I'm really not. I don't want this to sound like I'm above other gay men, even though I clearly am. But gay men are disgusting. And not disgusting in the sexy depraved sort of way because I very much enjoy that kind of disgusting – I mean, gay men are actually disgusting. They are either horrible friends, or they don't even let themselves become your friend. And I know some people will think I'm a bad gay for saying all these things out loud. But the truth is, I'm not a bad gay. Because I'm literally the best fucking gay you could ever possibly imagine. I'm intimidating – in a good way. I have the shrill voice of a fisherman's wife. I have gorgeous skin. I pretend to be interested in fashion.
I pretend to like going to the theatre to see a problematic play that literally no one asked for. I have a sense of humour that transcends and exceeds the wit of every other person in the room I find myself in. And clothes look really fucking good on me. I'm literally a better gay man than Cher.

It's just I truly believe they're terrified of me. Other gay men – they're actually terrified of me. I think I remind them of their own gayness, and I think more gay men than you realise secretly wish they weren't so gay. Which is why they choose to be wary of someone like me who just can't help being a big fat gay. They can't stand someone like me because they can't stand someone who's just like them. And I suppose that's why I can't bring myself to hate them back. Dominic and David and Daniel are probably just as awkward and horny and worried and paranoid and sad as I am – they just have a really shitty way of showing that sadness. And I really wish cunts like them could learn to be kinder to themselves because then they just might start being kinder to people like me.

Because people like me make great friends. Like, seriously, I'm a great friend... as well as great marriage material. It's not just my good skin that makes me alright to be around either. I know what I'm talking about, for a start. And I'm a right fucking laugh.

Thomas sent a photo
by William Dalrymple

Thomas   First off, we call them nudes, Gran. I'm so sorry
you saw them and so glad you have cataracts, but it
was an accident.

Of course it was an accident!

I'm lucky you didn't drop dead of a heart attack.

Oh. Next Tuesday? Well. Good luck. These days it's
basically an outpatient procedure so I wouldn't
worry.

You're in my contacts as 'Gran' – obviously – and
my friend Graham, who was *supposed* to get the
pictures –

He's in his twenties.

I know, but he's still called Graham. The fact that
Grandad was also called Graham is nothing more
than a horrible coincidence.

Twenty-eight! Two years older. I *knew* this would –

I'm not shouting! Well, I am. But that's because you
won't wear your hearing aid.

For a 91 year old? Yes, you're handling this extremely well. Apart from the aortic murmur. Again, good
luck in surgery.

Nudes. The other men in the pictures are nude.

I dunno, everyone's at it. You send nudes to someone because... well, you just do. It's like shaking hands.

Or other parts of the body, yes. In the bath. He had my permission to do that.

I mean, often that *is* what we do when *we* meet a man for the first time, but I take your point.

The first one? That's not a nude; if you put your readers on you'll be able to make out the speedos.

I wish I'd just sent that one too. His name is Callum. He's very polite and he polishes his shoes. You'd love him.

Not a 'friend', as such. We've been on a couple of dates. I wanted Graham's opinion. Graham and I have swapped nudes, yeah, but I don't really look at them anymore. It's like when they show old *Countdown*s on telly. Seen it all before.

I don't know why, really. I've never...

It's a good question, Gran. Maybe we send nudes to each other because it *is* like shaking hands. Because that's what you do when you don't know someone. Because you have to start somewhere. And we don't know where to start. We've never known. Why would we? We all spent all those years using only our eyes. Longing in absolute silence. If you make it past the nudes, if there's something to share besides your genitalia, if a handshake turns into a hug, then you know you're onto something. But what are the chances of that?

What? Oh for god's sake. Wear your bloody hearing

aid, Gran! You just missed an incredibly moving speech about the homosexual experience.

No, no, it's alright. I'm still glad you called. And to answer your first question: yes, I am gay.

Turkey and Ribs
by Lantian Chen

Note on the Chinese delivery: if the line '我是同性恋。' is too hard, it can be skipped. 'Ma', the reference of mother, should keep the Mandarin tone of the Chinese character '妈'.

Jason Si-Cheng Liang (梁思诚)   Yes, it's a penis. It's Elliot's penis. Why are you looking at my phone? (*Snatches his phone*) Give me, ma!

Because he wants me to see it. Because I want to see it. Because Elliot is not my *friend*. He's my boyfriend and we like looking at each other's dicks. You don't believe it?

(*Scrolling*)

You want to see mine too?

(*Shows her*)

Why the face – you've seen it before! You made it! And Elliot *loves* it. He likes to *suck* it and take it into his *ass* –

Gets a slap in the face. The phone flies out of his hand. He doesn't retrieve it.

THIS IS WHY I JOINED HIS FAMILY FOR THANKSGIVING! You really believed I stayed on campus for extra research? It was goddamn Thanksgiving. And I chose to stay with Elliot because he's my *boyfriend*, and his parents are really *nice* people!

What are you doing? Are you crying? You never cry!

I really wanted it to be the other way, ma. To invite Elliot to ours. For him to meet you. For you to get to know him.

Truth is, turkey tastes like shit. I *also* don't understand why *that* is reserved for the big American holiday. I kept thinking about your pork ribs. Wishing I could see Elliot's face when he took his first bite. He'd stay at our house forever. I could show him how to blend the rice with the sauce.

Elliot's house was so big, so intimidating, so... calming. Their puppy Napoleon playing under our dinner table. His dad asked me how we met. I told him about seeing Elliot for the first time in the American History class. His mom said we should dress nicer, at least we shouldn't be beat by straight Harvard boys. Laughter. So strange. I felt I could actually be *me*.

Of course. I am such an ungrateful and horrible person, I know. As you've said so many times. And now I *have to* be. Because I am gay. Ma, look at me. I am *gay*. 我是同性恋。

Don't go ma... please, don't... I love you ma. All I've ever wanted is to make you happy. And that's killing me every day.

I can't fix this. This is something beyond me. Beyond *us*. Believe me, I've tried. For seven whole years I was trying to make this part of me disappear. I thought I had to make my mother proud, the woman who moved to this country on her own and learned to speak fluent English. I forced myself to jerk off watching women in porn. All that made me do is want to jump off a – Before Elliot (*chokes up*) I'd been trying so hard. All alone.

That time I saw those motherfuckers in middle school chasing another gay boy. 'Faggot! FAGGOT!' Catching him. Each one taking a piss on him! While we all stood watching and did nothing. I tried to tell you. I said, 'Some kids at school are really scary.' And you said,

'Just keep your head down and your nose in the books and no one will bother you.'

So I did just that. All the way to Harvard. All the way to the love of my life.

White. Rhodes Scholar. Varsity crew team. Harvard donor parents – he's basically a billionaire Pete

Buttigieg. Oh, he even wants three kids. (*Beat.*) But he'll never be enough for you, because he is a man. A man who I love despite these symbols, not because of them. Admit it, ma. You don't love me. You never did. You don't even know who I am.

Turner Prize
by Aaron Bowater

MARK: male, late 20s, middle class. Employed nine to five in middle management but really 'going places'. Think 'normal' but ambitious. Painfully 'normal'.

Mark   Did I ever tell you what they used to call me, that summer in Rome? 'Mr. Turner'.

No, Rory. Nothing to do with the painter. I wish. They used to call me Mr. Turner because I only slept with 'straight' men.

Yes well... straight*ish*.

(Exasperated) That was the best fucking year of my life, until you turned up. One year – one year of getting stupidly drunk and stupidly gay. Not that I'm in the closet now of course. No. Everybody knows I'm gay.

No – sorry – 'not straight.' I prefer 'not straight' – provides some much-needed wiggle room, doesn't it? And unlike you, I actually need the wiggle room. You don't need any because you are a bullshitter.

It's not like I've make any great effort to hide anything.

And as for Megan? Yes, we were dating at the time. And yes, she is now my wife. She knows everything.

Don't panic. Not *everything*. But everything else. She even knows the old nickname.

Oh yes, she knows that I'm not straight and that I have had one or two gay experiences.

She obviously doesn't think one or two is a literal numerical record.

Without her I don't think I'd be out. She made me feel so normal. So comfortable. Then, 'cause of her, I met... you.

The rest of them... Well, the rest of them I've already forgotten. They never meant anything. Without fail I would lose interest the moment they reciprocated or the second I finished.

Do you know... I'll never forget that night I bumped into you in that bar. I'd been in Rome months. Why didn't you tell me you were there? And don't pretend it was to avoid me because you could have avoided me – *really* avoided me if you'd wanted to.

I'll never forgive you.

Do you remember what I said to you when you made your move? I told you to fuck off. Do you remember what you said? Nothing. Just fucking laughed as if... us... me... was nothing. Just a big fucking joke.

Beat.

That next day was the best day of my life. Waking up next to you. I could have fucking cried. How gay is that? I wish I had done. Might have made you realise that something had happened. Fuck knows what that 'something' was.

Flash of anger and contempt.

Fuck knows what's going on in your head. If anything is going on in your head... Let's face it you've never been much of a thinker.

My hand on your midriff, and that was it. You woke up.

You flew back to England the next day. And for the past fuck knows how many months, years even, we've just carried on. You know everybody knows? Well, they don't know *everything* but they aren't fucking stupid. Though we have gotten pretty good at hiding in plain sight.

Sighs. Resigned.

Still, it was good of you to be a groomsman. Not my idea. Hers. Do you know what she said?

'Well, if my sisters are all bridesmaids... my brother needs to be in there somewhere.'

Indeed you fucking do.

Vada the Bona Eke
by Bobby Harding

January 25th 1987. It's early hours the morning after the Royal Vauxhall Tavern was violently raided by 35 police officers in gloves. KYLE and his friend Dennis are in a holding cell. Kyle is a proper East London queen, fiery but with a heart of gold.

KYLE   You know the Tavern had to give 'em all their measures. The whole fuckin' jar! Those queens saved up for months and for what? For the Lillies to go and spend it on prozzies and fogus?
It was that fucking closet sharpy, I bet yous anything they was askin' too many questions at the station and he ratted on us to prove he weren't a fruit. If he tries to tie anything to me I swear to Gloria and all her saints I'll grass that camp little rozzer up. *[beat]* It's getting worse, Den, every time I go out I see me own blood mixed in with other folks' tricklin' down the pavement into the gutter. Council don't even clean it, won't touch bold blood. They just leave it, like a rotting, brown stamp to remind us where we belong. Same with the stamps they print all over yer eke; takes a whole schooner of slap just to get through the next day at work nishta questions. *[beat]* Summit's gonna snap soon. They think they can keep on beatin' and arrestin' folk like nothing'll ever happen? Think we're nellies, but we won't take

it much longer. Mark my words they'll doza the wrong fucking queen and then this boiling pot's gonna blow and I wanna be right in there when it does. Smash a pig onk or two. They all fucking deserve it and I'm fucking sick of pretending they don't. FASCISTS! *[to an approaching guard]* All except you ducky! *[back to Dennis]* 'Sides if worse comes to worse these lallies'll be too quick for 'em... I was just a kush bevvied... this time. God, Den, I wish someone would park us a vogue I'm rattlin'. Bugger my right to a call, it should be a faggot's right to a smoke. *[chuckle]* Bona we've got each other ain't it, doll?

Glossary:

Vada – Behold/Look	*Bona – Good*
Eke – Face	*Measures – Money*
Queens – Older gays	*Lillies – Police*
Fogus – Tobacco	*Closet – Not out*
Sharpy – Policeman	*Fruit – Gay man*
Gloria – God	*Rozzer – Policeman*
Folk – Queer people	*Bold – Gay*
Schooner – Bottle	*Slap – Makeup*
Nishta – No/Nothing	*Nelly – Weak*
Doza – Kill (Ferricadoza)	*Onk – Nose*
Lallies – Feet	*Bevvied – Drunk*
Kush – Slight/Bit	*Park – Give*
Vogue – Cigarette	*Rattlin – Shaking*
Doll – Pretty	

What Do You Think of This?
by Will Armstrong

CONNOR   Okay son, what do you think of *this*. A
traditional kids' magic show, in a club for gay men.

Ahtatatata, hold it, stay out here a second! This is a
fantastic idea.

If we do this together, we could hit your demo-
graphic, right. Start small, touring around bars like
that one you snuck out to sometimes, remember,
what was it called... was it The Cum-something, no,
The Knobstacle Course! Yes, well they like this drag
stuff, they like blue gags, so we do my old kids'
party routines but we *modernise* them so they work
for your crowd. Yeah?

I could do it in a bloody tutu. I know! Me! I must
be crackers, but I will admit, your mother left a
mascara behind in a drawer, and I'll admit to you
now, I did have a go and I was, I mean it looked
alright, it did!

Seriously son, all the old props are interchange-
able. You've got the magic wand you give to kids
and it breaks into pieces in their hand, and then you
know you hold it and it's stiff as a *[international sign
language for cock]*... see! It writes itself. You shove

186

the trick wand inside a rubber whatsit and all of a sudden you can use it at the clubs for you know, where the drag queens go, it is funny! We could pull a rabbit out of a hat, but it's dressed like, I dunno, Janet Jackson? This is a fantastic idea. I'm seeing these things a lot clearer now I've, you know, given it up. And card tricks are a bit *[international sign language for queer]* anyway? I mean I don't want to, obviously, say anything *wrong* but you know, they are.

Because I've watched it all, I've read up, I know this is what your lot likes, and I get it now. Us touring around, it'd be no different to when you were a sprog and you used to come out with me and help with the magic at the little birthday parties! You knew how all the tricks set up, we'd have a laugh doing it, I think about it all the time. You were great, you used to make all the kids scream laughing, and when you did your face would light up like Christmas, honestly you were born to make people feel... joy.

I'm sure you're *really* busy, being a 'male nurse', but at least think about giving this a chance. I love you, you know that, you're my son and you're a great man. And I am too, now, and I know you probably doubt that a lot of the time, but things have changed. Before... that wasn't the real me, you see that. Well you should see that, for fuck's sake I mean I'm, I'm basically begging you here aren't I, look at me. Look at me. And please try not to fucking judge me for once in your life, when I'm the one pulling the weight here. I mean if we're being perfectly straight... *[mockingly woke]* no offence Adam... how can you, now, on purpose, put me through what I must have... done to you? Hmm? How dare you do that to me. *You* must know what it's like, people leaving. You must know how that feels.

So do this act. With me. Please.